E N G A G I N G

TEACHERS

Metro Instructional Supp Lab
School of Education, PSU-ED
P.O. Box 751
Portland, OR 97207-0751

ENGAGING

TEACHERS

Creating

Teaching/Researching

Relationships

Edited by
Betty Shockley Bisplinghoff
JoBeth Allen

Foreword by Brenda Power

Heinemann
Portsmouth, NH

Heinemann
A division of Reed Elsevier Inc.
361 Hanover Street
Portsmouth, NH 03801-3912
Offices and agents throughout the world.

We would like to thank those who have given their permission to include material in this book.

Funding for the School Research Consortium was provided by the National Reading Research Center of the University of Georgia and the University of Maryland under the Educational Research and Development Centers Program (PR?Award#117A20007) as administered by the Office of Educational Research and Improvement, U.S. Department of Education. The opinions expressed here do not necessarily reflect the position of policies of the NRRC, OERI, or the USDE.

Cataloging-in-Publications Data is on file at the Library of Congress.

ISBN: 0-325-00037-9

Editor: Bill Varner
Cover design: Darci Mehall
Manufacturing: Louise Richardson
Printed in the United States of America on acid-free paper.
00 99 98 EB 1 2 3 4 5

CONTENTS

FOREWORD

Recently I sat with a small group of teacher researchers from throughout the country. We were disagreeing about whether teacher researchers needed to take their work to larger audiences, through publications or presentations. Finally one of the teachers said, "For me, it's like if Michaelangelo chose to paint the mural on his bedroom ceiling instead of in the Sistine Chapel. I mean, it would still be great art. But . . . who would see it in his bedroom?" Everyone laughed, and we immediately had a new perspective for considering the issue.

I think of this analogy when I look at the work of Betty Shockley Bisplinghoff and JoBeth Allen. Much teacher research is relational, situated in specific contexts, and of most interest to those directly involved in it. How do you take the personal to the public realm? Yet at the same time, teacher researchers have begun to transform the way we think about educational reform, and teachers' work in it. This transformation can only occur when teacher research processes and practices are made public.

In this remarkable book, Betty and JoBeth bring together the experiences and insights of many teachers they have worked with, involved in the most difficult aspect of teacher research—learning to work in research communities with others. These essays are an honest and unvarnished view of the tensions that emerge between teachers on their turf and university guests, the problems involved in balancing teaching and research agendas, the conflicts that need to be negotiated as groups of teachers find their own way into the research questions that matter most to them.

Betty, JoBeth, and their co-authors are able to explore the depths of these issues because they never lose their sense of humor or their respect for the communities they work in. This book is the third in the trilogy that includes *Engaging Children* and *Engaging Families*, and it presents the same vision of teacher research set forth in the previous books (co-authored with Barbara Michalove). In all these books, the research agendas emerge as teachers, children, and families build plans and develop research strategies based upon their shared commitment to helping the students in their care.

The teacher research movement is growing, and moving in many directions. At its best, the movement does have the ability to transform the profession. But at its worst, it can be self-indulgent on two levels. Teachers can use research strategies merely to reinforce and celebrate what they are already doing well, instead of pushing themselves, through research, to improve practice. Or even worse, the researcher can be self-indulgent in her work, acknowledging and considering only her own development through endless analysis of personal journals and feelings—the research equivalent of picking the lint out of the classroom's belly button.

Betty and JoBeth's work is a model for others who would assist teacher researchers in finding their way. Though their guidance and intervention is essential to the work of these teachers, they remain quietly in the background in much of the trilogy. They don't need to trumpet the value of teacher research or their work as facilitators—it's clearly evident in the ways teachers, students, and curriculums in these classrooms change.

I have used books in the *Engaging* series for four years in my teacher research graduate courses, and they are always favorites of my students. The testament to the power of these books is how much teachers change both their practice, and their views of research by reading them. Many parents in Maine now exchange journals with their child's teacher as a direct result of Betty and JoBeth's work. Even more important than the journal exchange, the teacher's view of the child in these journals is infused with a respect inspired by the respectful tone of teacher researchers who work with Betty and JoBeth.

While the *Engaging* series has changed teaching practices, ultimately I think the greatest contribution will be in reconceiving research strategies. I used to think the highest compliment I could give to an author was to say they wrote things I didn't have the courage to say. I realized early on with the *Engaging* series that Betty and JoBeth write things about research techniques I haven't the courage to think. For example, in one passage from the *Engaging Families* book, they wrote about carefully categorizing their data. I nodded my head in agreement, thinking here was a wonderful example of how systematic and careful teacher researchers were in their work. And then on the next page, they reflected upon how this systematic, by-the-book analysis was distancing them from the data and not useful for them. They abandoned the traditional analysis method, and instead went on a writer's retreat filled with delicious food, long walks on the beach, and fruitful talks. This is a truly radical notion of what makes for good research analysis and writing, and only this level of honesty will help teachers discover the research methods that can work best for them.

In the analogy of Michaelangelo's painting, the lesson is clear—great work needs a wide audience. The lessons from the *Engaging* series run much deeper, and are more complex. Betty and JoBeth show with humor and grace how the private and personal tensions and discoveries of teacher research can be made public. Teacher researchers need to learn how to present their research processes as well as the findings from their work. We need more stories of how research communities emerge and are supported over time. These are relational and local issues that have global implications for all teacher researchers. It's bedroom talk needed in a public chapel, and that's the just-right, unique tone of *Engaging Teachers*. This is a book that will rest on the nightstand of many teachers, quietly inspiring new ways of thinking about research in their lives, and their relationships with other teachers. And in those still, private moments, very public changes in curriculum and school communities will be born.

—Brenda Power

ENGAGING

TEACHERS

ONE

Developing the Habits
of Organic Inquiry

Betty Shockley Bisplinghoff

This is a book about change. It's a little book with a reasonable message about how research and teaching can be supportive partners. It recognizes teaching as more of a lifestyle than a day job and presents research as a complementary state of mind. Instead of adding research onto our already too heavy workloads, we offer a "take charge" look at opportunities for a more organic union between this life work of teaching and the mental work of continuing to learn.

JoBeth Allen and I have spent almost ten years learning together, drawing on our different professional lifestyles of university professor (teacher) and elementary school teacher to help us better understand ourselves and our work. When my school faculty became interested in changing the way reading was addressed at our school, JoBeth was there to join us as a long-term consultant. We soon began to wonder what our change to more holistic practices would mean for the literacy development of the children we worried about the most. Along with second-grade teacher Barbara Michalove (our longtime co-researcher), we identified six children and studied their responses to our decisions to offer choices in reading and writing, extended time to read and write, more and varied response opportunities, and membership in a class community where literate activities were central. This four-year study, *Engaging Children: Community and Chaos in the Lives of Young Literacy Learners* (Allen, Michalove, and Shockley 1993), taught us much about the literacy development of struggling students. It also led us into our next study.

We came to realize how our understanding of student learning is limited without the input of children's first teachers, their parents. We knew from discussions with the children that their families were very influential in the ways they used literacy in their own lives, and the varied ways they supported their children's literacy development. We knew our insights would have been much richer with the perspectives of parents and other family members. Recognizing most specifically the need to nurture better home and school communication networks, the three of us studied the parallel practices that I created and Barbara modified for the students and families the next year. We wrote about the fascinating connections among children, family members, teachers, and literature in *Engaging Families: Connecting Home and School Literacy Communities*.

Working so closely with students that worried me the most, joining with families to study home/school partnerships, and building a research relationship with a school colleague and a university colleague showed me that looking at issues from multiple perspectives can enrich practice and stimulate thinking. That belief led to my facilitation of a new group of teachers who came together to learn through researching their own classroom issues. In *Engaging Teachers*, the final book in the series, we share research issues and experiences, problems and possibilities. In three years together, this new community of researchers learned that teaching is as much about learning as knowing, and that research may offer us a rich and rigorous route to new understanding. This group, many engaging in teacher research for the first time, struggled to unite teaching and research, an ongoing challenge even to those of us who have been "engaged" for many years.

Becoming Engaged by Teacher Research

The contributors to this volume are teachers in the Athens, Georgia area who formed the School Research Consortium (SRC). With support from the National Reading Research Center (NRRC) at the University of Georgia, we came together to explore how and if research works to enhance teaching and learning. For some, it was an extension of practice that met a real need; for others, it wasn't. It seemed to work best for those who came to believe that teachers can decide for themselves what counts as research and for those who found ways to connect that research to methods that were part of who they were and how they learned as teachers. By experimenting with uniting teaching and research, we came to appreciate Aunt Dot's thinking in Dorothy Allison's memoir *Two or Three Things I Know for Sure*:

> "Lord, girl, there's only two or three things I know for sure." She put her head back, grinned, and made a small impatient noise. Her eyes glittered as bright as sun reflecting off the scales of a cottonmouth's back. She spat once and shrugged. "Only two or three things. That's right," she said. "Of course it's never the same things, and I'm never as sure as I'd like to be." (1995, 5)

We no longer think there is one sure way to do research, any more than there is one sure way to teach. Research still won't make us as sure as we'd like to be, but it will help us act with a new level of confidence that our decisions are based on data from our classrooms and our students, thoughtfully collected and considered by us. Research reteaches us how having questions can be a good thing.

Most basically, having a question to pursue can actually give us some relief from the pressures of teaching in settings that are always accruing new requirements and mandates for this new program and that next initiative. Our research is ours. It can be a stabilizing feature of our work. It helps us filter the maze of demands we always seem to be facing.

I recently met a teacher who was feeling very frustrated by the number of reform initiatives adopted by her school. They were trying to implement portfolio assessment, site-based management, working regularly with Columbia University professors to improve their writing instruction, as well as working through other curricular changes. She described her situation as being similar to a bunch of can-dles floating in a bowl where each initiative floats alone, never joining to form a single, stronger flame. This teacher had a strong desire to learn more about reader response but never got to it because everything else took up her time. She said she had stacks of journals and books in her house that she never actually read because she couldn't decide on a place to start. Now, through conversations with other teacher researchers, she has taken control of her professional life. She decided to spend the rest of the year learning about reader response theory and seeing how what other researchers have written matches what her students are doing. She plans to develop reader response portfolios with her students and to encourage more thoughtful writing patterns through this medium. She is determined to learn in a manner that is meaningful, both to her and to her students.

For this teacher, as well as to us in the SRC, thinking of ourselves as teacher researchers generated a recognition of teaching and learning habits that became critical to classroom research. Deborah Meir (1995) wrote about her faculty's de-velopment of its "intellectual habits of mind" in *The Power of Their Ideas*:

> It was all very well to refer to "habits of mind," but the phrase seemed too abstract. We didn't want an endless laundry list either, so we wrote down five. . . . We . . . remind ourselves and the world that they weren't handed to us from Above. We never quite write them out the exact same way, and over the years we've realized they are con-stantly evolving in their meaning. They are: the question of evidence, or "How do we know what we know?"; the question of viewpoint in all its multiplicity, or "Who's speaking?"; the search for connections and patterns, or "What causes what?"; supposi-tion, or "How might things have been different?"; and finally, why any of it matters, or "Who cares?" (p. 49)

When our community of teacher researchers (SRC) opened our minds to ac-cept this kind of flexible yet rigorous learning, and believed that research methods were not handed down from "Above," we surprised ourselves with our discover-ies. Karen Hankins (Chapter 2) has been developing a new habit of mind, an in-tensely personal answer to "How do I know what I know?" The "evidence" she found came through connecting her life and the lives of her students. Karen ex-plored these connections in a reflective journal. This was not a journal she decided to keep the day she renamed herself a teacher researcher. Journaling had been a natural part of her way of learning for years. In fact, it was through a process of reinterpreting entries from long ago that Karen was able to make sense of events in her kindergarten classroom. Memoir became method and research became organic to Karen's teaching. She had a focus—how to support the learning of three alco-hol/crack-affected students in her classroom—and she had a method that fit not only her question but also her life.

In their three-generation memoir, *Childtimes* (1979), Eloise Greenfield and Lessie Jones Little report the words of Pattie Frances Ridley Jones, their mother and grandmother:

> Memory is a funny thing. You never know how it's going to act. A lot of things that I saw and heard, and heard about, when I was a girl, I can't call to mind at all now. My memory just hop-skips right over them. Some other things, I can almost remember, but

when I try to catch hold of them, they get mixed up with something else, or disappear. But then, there are the things that keep coming back, keep coming back just as plain, just as clear. . . . (p. 7)

Karen teaches us to pay attention to both the hops and skips of our histories as well as what comes back plain and clear. If we do, our teaching and our research will be the richer for it.

Teachers at Comer Elementary School (Chapter 3) were surprised by how good research could feel one year and how bad the next. They learned the difference between research that feels imposed versus research that is generative—emerging from personally assessed needs and genuine interests. When their research team decided to experience writing for themselves first-hand, they were excited by their work and stimulated by their efforts. They felt they would learn more about how to help their students as writers by going through the process themselves. When they thought they had to implement phase two of their project the next year even though they were not ready to do so, they felt pressured and defeated.

A research orientation can be fragile if it is not integral to current needs and practices, if it is not organic. Hubbard and Power (1993) recognized this critical element in their handbook for teacher researchers. They suggest that teachers ask, "How can the data-collection and analysis procedures be as much a part as possible of the 'organic whole' of the class? . . . Teachers who are conducting research in the midst of their teaching work to find ways to collect their data within the structure of their classroom schedule and activities" (p. 55). Sylvia Ashton Warner, author of *Teacher* (1963) and originator of the term "organic reading," wrote,

First words must have intense meaning.
First words must be already part of the dynamic life.
First books must be made of the stuff of the child himself, whatever and wherever the child.

Like "first words," teacher research must have intense meaning for each participant. It too must be part of the dynamic life of a teacher's particular classroom context. And methods of study must be made of the stuff of the researcher herself and the group of students with whom s/he works. When this opportunity to learn is inclusive in the sense that anyone can enter the discourse wherever he or she is, with no prior "training" in a particular research tradition required, then new ways of learning and knowing can emerge more organically from the stuff of daily praxis and living.

As a teacher researcher, I had to develop my own style; so too has each SRC member. In the preface to *Teacher*, Herbert Read wrote, "There are many possible approaches to creative education, but they all usually fail because they are too intentional, too self-consciously applied. Miss Ashton-Warner has realized that teaching is an organic process" (p. 12). She believed in simplicity. As teacher researchers we must embrace this kind of organic simplicity.

Teacher research is a delicate balance between using what you think you know and learning as you go. It's a seesaw ride. Too often the idea of adding research to the already demanding work of teaching feels thrust upon us. It seems much bigger than we are. Then research rests so heavy that it knocks us off balance and we fly off the other end of our seesaw, claiming research is no longer our friend and we're not going to play with it any more. In other instances, the expectation of research as a partner for teaching has little personal value. It is something for the whole school to tackle, and so you choose to rest your end of the seesaw on the ground while somewhere out there a school-wide initiative takes shape that one day will require you to push off and contribute your data to the growing form at the other end.

But at its best, teaching and research feel so balanced that each supports the other, like the seesaw partner at the playground who has only to move a little up or back to achieve that searched-for stillness, no feet touching. In the real life of research and teaching, the daily ups and downs of learning with others are noted by some form of record keeping, reflected on and balanced by a shift in strategies. When that recording, reflecting, and shifting meshes, there's a calm about it, a graceful movement between teaching and research.

A Little History

In the fall of 1992, a committee of three school-based researchers (Barbara Michalove, Valerie Garfield, and myself) and two university-based researchers (JoBeth Allen and Jim Baumann) worked together to create a School Research Consortium. The university researchers who wrote the initial proposal seeking support from the National Reading Research Center realized that something new was needed to connect theory and practice in ways that would be meaningful to teachers. The NRRC was funded for five years (1992-1997) by the U.S Department of Education, Office of Educational Research and Improvement (OERI). The grant to support teacher research was historic because never before had a federally funded research and development center tried to ground theory in practice in this manner.

The committee sent a letter to all public elementary and secondary schools within 30 miles of the University of Georgia campus, inviting school faculties to discuss their most pressing literacy concerns. The SRC committee then listened to research ideas from interested faculty at thirteen schools. On the basis of these meetings, the SRC committee encouraged faculties as well as individual teachers to identify in writing their own research questions and their expectations for a university/school collaboration. The preliminary research questions evolved into the more formal research projects approved by OERI (see appendix A). The proposal process was repeated again for the next year; most members continued with related questions, some were not able to stay in the SRC, and some new members joined. The final year centered on trying to understand what we've been learning along the way through writing *Engaging Teachers*.

In a National Reading Conference presentation (1995), SRC members shared their reactions to that initial invitation to join the SRC. Ann Keffer confessed,

> I remember hearing about the SRC . . . when our principal read us their letter and asked us if any of us were interested enough to have some representatives come out

and speak to us, and some of us were, and they did . . . So they talked about forming research partnerships and having teachers take a more active role in research. What interests me at this point is how difficult it was for me then to believe them. I assumed that they wanted to use my students as research subjects and this time they wanted me to do some of the work for them . . . Then, it turned out that what they really wanted was for us to look for answers to our own questions. . . .

Dera Weaver, another member of the SRC, told the audience about another way in which teachers can be discouraged,

Teachers are screened from the kinds of things that they might want to be participating in. Maybe my principal never got the letter. I don't know . . . I heard about it through the grapevine. I'd like to be in on this but my principal needs to approve it so there was an awkwardness in that. And I think that is a story of teachers' access in general to the world of research. It's not even enough to be asked. Someone has to say yes, you can go to the prom.

Claiming Our Way

Once we came together as a school research consortium, we had more to come to terms with. How does a group dedicated to finding personally sensitive ways to enhance knowing negotiate the requirements of a governmental agency that already knew what they counted as research? The following sections tell the story of how we tried to find our way amidst the competing demands of OERI, NRRC, school and district requirements, our personal lives, and our primary responsibility, the students. One of the first challenges was trying to decide what we thought teacher research was and what others expected from us. The Teachers as Writers team from Comer Elementary School described their concerns at the time (Carr 1994):

We thought they'd [SRC Coordinators] tell us what research to do with a professor or graduate students. When they didn't, we almost bowed out and said, "Go find someone who knows how to do research." But we didn't, because they think teachers are the ones who should be doing research.

It was difficult to rid ourselves of the idea that other people knew better than we did what we should be doing as researchers. That whole first year we kept trying to accommodate other people's definitions of what real research was. We stood in our classrooms trying on method after method, but the methods always seemed too large or too small, rarely just right. We always seemed to be wearing someone else's model, hoping for that tailored fit. Some of us tried to make quantitative methods fit our complex and ever changing environments and felt like we were being squeezed into a too small suit. Some tried to adhere to qualitative traditions only to find that the cloak of the ethnographer did not always fit a teacher either. We needed to look in the mirror and take notice of the existing fabric of our lives. What kinds of records were we already keeping? What additional information would enhance ways we already had for learning about ourselves and our students? How could we use the time we had with our students to understand learning opportunities from their perspectives? We were surrounded with potential, but it was still hard to see in that mirror anything other than what we had been trained to see.

Certainly we struggled most with freeing ourselves from a limited definition of research. As Keffer et al. (Chapter 3) explain so eloquently, many SRC members originally "doubted our competence," especially when defining research as experimental design, and analysis as statistical. "Our best insights," they discovered, "came from observing and documenting our daily process." One member of that team, Debby Wood, in keeping with the Central Park East "habits of mind," came to a new understanding of teacher research:

> You have a question, you're willing to document the process you go through [to answer it], and you're willing to share it in the end. That's what people need—people who will share their stories . . . It's important that this kind of work comes from us, comes from teachers who are really teaching children and know. (Keffer, Carr, Lanier, Mattison, Wood, and Stanulis 1996)

Researchers Carol and John Santa (1995) wrote "that a reflective attitude is the hallmark of good teaching, but not all good teaching involves a research attitude" (p. 443). Developing a "research attitude" meant, for most of us, first developing a better attitude toward research. Shelley Carr expressed her broadening view of research and her development of a research attitude as, "I'm just kind of listening better [to my students] and I'm asking myself questions in my head that I probably wouldn't have if we hadn't started this." It is a purposeful research attitude that we wanted to nurture, something beyond the reflective moment, a line of thought to be pursued in a passionate and integrated manner. We were becoming inspired teacher researchers. So much so that Shelley later added, "I now have a migraine of ideas."

Another way change was occurring was in our increasing commitment to the habit of mind that asks, "Who's speaking?" We began to seek that multiplicity of viewpoints that would give voice to parents, students, and colleagues. It was important to listen to and trust our own voices first, but as we did, we became increasingly tuned in to the harmonies and discords within and beyond our classrooms. As facilitators of the SRC, JoBeth Allen and I had the opportunity to look across the group and reflect on expansion of the classroom walls (Chapter 6).

In her novel *These Same Long Bones*, Gwendolyn Parker contemplates the difficult process of viewing the world, and making decisions, by considering multiple viewpoints.

> It was never simple when you had to gather up what people were saying and add in all that you knew. That was always hard and a challenge, hard because sometimes what you knew was hard, and a challenge because sometimes other people didn't want to see what you saw. What people would let themselves see came in layers, and even your own knowing could weave in and out of itself. And then there were the things people refused to think about at all, things that would surprise them later, things they might even regret. (p. 174)

Change was occurring, but it was happening slowly against a backdrop of conflicts with the needs and requirements of OERI and NRRC. From the beginning, our affiliations with OERI and NRRC were both a support and a constraint.

Because we had some financial backing, we were able to hire substitutes in order to have release days from school once every other month, and to pay for research-related expenses such as photocopying student work, buying professional books, subscribing to professional journals, and purchasing technical equipment such as tape recorders. But the requirements to write research proposals in the language and form of university and government institutions, to conform to a March-to-March fiscal year schedule that was so out of sync with our school calendars, and to write annual reports for each project kept the pressure of writing uncomfortably close for people who wanted and needed to spend time developing appropriate methods first. These structures were someone else's, not our own, and the limitations they placed on us were often nonsensical, causing most of us to question our commitments to teacher research. What we most needed was the kind of support identified by Seymour Papert, author of *The Children's Machine* (1993): "The problem for society is to give teachers the same pluralist support that the best of them give their students. Individuals at different places need support to move from where they are. They cannot be cajoled or ordered into a too distant place" (p. 81). Many times it seemed, the place where OERI or NRRC wanted us to be was very distant from where we felt we really were. We needed support from the established researchers at OERI and NRRC for Papert's observation that "In education, the highest mark of success is not having imitators but inspiring others to do something else" (p. 78).

The poet Quincy Troupe (1994) explained that "Language is culturally specific. It comes from out of a place. You must write from where you come from." We not only believe we can write from this place, our teaching place; we also believe we can be "real researchers" right where we are. Our research comes out of our relationships with our pasts and our present, our relationships with our students and each other. Novel insights can come from the hard but satisfying work of examining our practices and their relationship to student learning. We no longer aim to discover THE best way to support our students on their varied paths toward literate participation in our democratic society. We see now that the questions are many and the answers will also be multiple. We have come to accept versions of research that are uniquely attuned to our specific situations. In other words, in both our teaching and our researching we have become more appreciative of the stance of Allison's Aunt Dot. We think we know "two or three things" for sure, but we're willing to change what we thought we knew "for sure" today based on our ongoing learning from our own research.

The teachers from Cedar Shoals High School (Chapter 5) operated from this stance. They looked at their curriculum and their students and asked, "How might things be different?" They examined the supposition that the authority to design curriculum lies in a hierarchy from state to district to teachers. They asked how learning might be different if it began with students. In the nearby Georgia mountains, Eliot Wigginton first risked giving his students the lead in creating their own learning in response to curriculum mandates. They found a place for themselves among other people's ideas and plans. The heretofore overlooked stories of people in their community led them to significant personal and public change. The Cedar Shoals researchers had studied Wigginton's Foxfire innovations and had often talked of incorporating his core practices into their work. Collaborative teacher research became an avenue to enact these changes. Their incorporation of state guidelines in more interactive classrooms through student generated curriculum honors the power of the Foxfire ideology, a belief system so universal that it can survive the mistakes of its fallen leader.

The Cedar Shoals teachers imagined school in a new way. With their students they created an alternative reality. Maxine Greene (1995) wrote, "Of all our cognitive capacities, imagination is the one that permits us to give credence to alternative realities. It allows us to break with the taken for granted, to set aside familiar distinctions and definitions" (p. 3). The teachers in this collection took the risk to imagine that they could participate as researchers in a world that was not always welcoming to them, and that they could include their students in this effort. Greene reminds us that it is critical for all of us, teachers and students, to grow beyond "the mechanical chain of routine behaviors. . . . All depends upon a breaking free, a leap, and then a question. I would like to claim that this is how learning happens and that the educative task is to create situations in which the young are moved to *begin* to ask, in all the tones of voice there are, 'Why?' (p. 6).

As several groups and individuals in the SRC learned, research does not always progress according to plans, nor does it always yield what one hopes to find. It is critical to ask "Why?" Georgiana Sumner, Johni Mathis, and Michelle Commeyras (Chapter 4) continued to ask why their study was not working. By looking at their data again and again, they generated surprising new understandings about their second- and eighth-grade student relationships. Without a research perspective, time, and the support of SRC colleagues, they would have concluded the project and the year with some very negative feelings. They would have missed an opportunity to become aware of how distance from an event and looking again at what you thought you already "knew for sure" could lead to important insights about the centrality of relationships to learning.

An Invitation

Kim Chernin (1983) reminisced on her writing of *In My Mother's House*,

> This kind of story never took you exactly in the same way to the same place twice and really, once you came to give the matter some thought, you couldn't speak of beginnings or endings, it was all a twisting and unraveling and turning back on itself with unexpected moments right in the middle of the most familiar scenes. (p. viii)

That is where most of us find ourselves today, "twisting and unraveling and turning back" on our experiences to see what they can offer us for tomorrow, a tomorrow when we try to begin yet again. There is no once-and-for-all in teacher research. With people like Maxine Greene and Aunt Dot by our sides, we know "There are always vacancies: there are always roads not taken, vistas not acknowledged. The search must be ongoing; the end can never be quite known" (Greene, p. 15). What we can continue to offer is "to interpret life from our situated standpoints, to try—over and over again—to begin" (Greene, p. 16).

In the setting down on the pages of a book, our stories gain a life and lose a life, both at the same time. It is hard to portray the realities of teacher research with just words. There are the faces of the children, the energy of the moments, the interruptions, the tugs and pulls of living life in schools that cannot adequately be recounted no matter how skilled the writer. But we know that without the effort the ideas will be certainly lost, swallowed up by time almost as quickly as they happen. Feminist theorist and educator Laurel Richardson (1994) maintains, "Writing is also a way of knowing—a method of discovery and analysis. By writing in different ways, we discover new aspects of our topic and our relationship to it" (p. 516).

At a most basic level, we have come to recognize and accept more fully the power of our place and our time. We are learning to use what we have available to us in more meaningful ways. Papert (1993) again seemed to speak for us:

> Every one of us has built up a stock of intuitive, empathic, common sense knowledge about learning. This knowledge comes into play when one recognizes something good about a learning experience without knowing the outcome. It seems obvious to me that every good teacher uses this kind of knowledge far more than test scores or other objective measurements in daily decisions about students. Perhaps the most important problem in education research is how to mobilize and strengthen such knowledge. One step toward strengthening it is to recognize it. The denial of personal intuitive knowledge has led to a profound split in thinking about learning . . . A second strategy for strengthening the personal side and breaking the stranglehold of the School side is to develop a methodology for reflection about cases of successful learning and especially about one's own best learning experiences. (pp. 28-29)

This book is a collection of experiences and insights from teachers who are developing "methodologies of reflection," who share their own best learning experiences. We try to look with honesty, doubt, commitment, and even humor; the final chapter by Ann Keffer addresses the role of the researcher and the researched in a charming yet pointed allegory. We are trying to make our research, from the questions to the methods to the "why it matters," organic to our teaching. We invite you to join us.

References

Allen, J., B. Michalove, and B. Shockley. 1993. *Engaging Children: Community and Chaos in the Lives of Young Literacy Learners*. Portsmouth, NH: Heinemann.

Allison, D. 1995. *Two or Three Things I Know for Sure*. New York: Penquin.

Ashton-Warner, S. 1963. *Teacher*. New York: Simon & Schuster.

Chernin, K. 1983. *In my Mother's House: A Daughter's Story*. New York: Harper Perennial.

Greene, M. 1995. *Releasing the Imagination: Essays on Education, the Arts, and Social Change*. San Francisco: Jossey Bass.

Greenfield, E. and L.J. Little. 1979. *Childtimes: A Three-generation Memoir*. New York: Harper Trophy.

Hubbard, R. and B. Power. 1993. *The Art of Classroom Inquiry*. Portsmouth NH: Heinemann.

Keffer, A., S. Carr, B. Lanier, L. Mattison, D. Wood, and R. D. Stanulis. 1996. "Teacher Researchers Discover Magic in Forming an Adult Writing Workshop." *Language Arts* 73: 113–121.

Meir, D. 1995. *The Power of Their Ideas*. Boston: Beacon Press.

Papert, S. 1993. *The Children's Machine: Rethinking School in the Age of the Computer*. New York: HarperCollins.

Parker, G. 1994. *These Same Long Bones*. New York: Penquin.

Richardson, L. 1994. "Writing: A Method of Inquiry." In *Handbook of Qualitative Research*, ed. N. Denzin and Y. Lincoln, 516-529. Thousand Oaks, CA: Sage.

Santa, C.M. and J.L. Santa. 1995. "Teacher as Researcher." *Journal of Reading Behavior* 27(3): 439–451.

Shockley, B., B. Michalove, and J. Allen. 1995. *Engaging Families: Connecting Home and School Literacy Communities*. Portsmouth, NH: Heinemann.

Troupe, Q. 1993. *Reeling in the Big Ones: Tales of Fishing and Literacy*. Paper presented at the National Reading Conference, Charleston.

TWO

Cacophony to Symphony: Memoirs in Teacher Research[1]

Karen Hankins

Whit Davis Elementary School

The room was filled with the chatter of writing workshop. Nat puzzled over two crayons in his hand, one of them blue, "Mrs. Hankins, ain't you had you a blue bicycle when you was a little-girl-teacher?" Nat had a way of naming me for what I was, always a teacher—or is it always a little girl? I answer his *now* question, remembering my *past* blue bicycle and a childhood story I had shared with the children recently.

Perhaps it was one of those tell-me-about-when-you-were-little moments that brought memoir to the forefront of my teaching journal. Perhaps it was the need to make some quiet sense of the rising cacophonous days with Nat, Loretta, and Rodney (all exposed in utero to crack cocaine or a damaging amount of alcohol). The original impetus is lost now but the number of written memoirs grew as the year went on. The past seemed to wrap itself around my immediate questions.

I kept a journal all year documenting the three children's entry to school. This chapter, first, shares from memoirs in the journal in an attempt to document the impact recording the past had on my teaching. Secondly, this chapter documents a bit of the struggle of a novice teacher/researcher to claim a voice in the definition of research. Above all it asserts that we are never free from the past and we are never out of the future. And it joins the "memoir boom" (Gornick 1996) of this decade. Thousands of people are writing memoirs out of a collective, perhaps unvoiced, need. It makes sense that it would have an impact on our work. Like Gornick I understand that it is not "what happened [to me] that matters; but what [I] was able to *make* of what happened."

Overture

> "My assumption is that the story of any one of us is in some measure the story of us all."
>
> —Frederick Buechner

---

1. A version of this chapter will appear in the Spring 1998 Harvard Educational Review. Reprinted here by permission.

"Persons who become master teachers are likely to do so because of a tacit under-standing of how to shape and reshape the materials of their craft . . ."

—Maxine Green

"Writing is really very simple; all you do is sit down at the typewriter and open a vein."

—Red Smith

The three quotes against each other may "sound" as the warm-up of a symphony orchestra sounds. Each instrument separately tunes up and runs its own independent agenda for a minute or two before coming to common purpose. Then, they make music!

Let me conduct you to the common purpose I hear in the statements. For me they represent the multiple focuses of this writing. First, I came to understand that the children whose lives seemed so distantly crafted from mine were "in some measure a story of [myself]." Secondly, understanding that helped me "to shape and reshape the materials of my craft" in order to teach them. Finally, it was in "opening the vein," in the composing and practicing process of soul, pen, and paper that I heard the symphony.

Allegro: Why Memoirs?

Journal Entry.

So, I keep this journal. It was easier when no one else knew or cared that I wrote. It's a teaching journal. It's a personal journal. It's a research journal. It's both a personal and teaching journal because John Dewey first and Lucy Calkins later taught me to reflect on my day and my life in the same breath. It's both a Teaching and Research journal because I no longer believe that teaching can be separated from research. (Perhaps it CAN be but it shouldn't be.) The question is . . . I guess . . . Can it be both Personal and Research journal? That's what people really want me to defend. But how can I tell people what my heart and head do together in my classroom? For instance, today at a conference I talked to someone about my study. She "listened" politely and patiently. When I finished she had only one question, "But . . . did it help them learn to read *better*?" I looked her square in the face and said, "yes." I think she meant—"there are no numbers."

I remember that night. I closed my journal and felt tears well up and spill slowly down my face. I wept for my answer because there was joy there. But more than that I cried over her question. I keep running into the feeling that because I'm a teacher, I'm doing research wrong. And in honesty I want to be heard by that woman and the others she represents. I have a problem being controlled by formulated text and vocabulary. I wondered if there was a place for this research, this story, told my way.

When I write in my journal, it serves in much the same capacity as learning to play the cello (something else new in my life). Journaling is akin to practice time, full of starts, stops, repeats. Practicing new music is a time when the written score rules the fingers, the eyes, the whole body. You practice knowing, indeed hoping, that no one hears. However, the only real drive to practice grows from the belief that someday someone will want to hear.

I kept the journal of the three target children privately knowing no one would read it, but hoping someday someone would want to know the essence of the notes recorded there. I wrote at nap time, waiting for faculty meeting to begin, the last ten minutes before turning out the light each night, or on the backs of church bulletins or napkins in restaurants. I had never heard of fieldnotes at the time. I read recently a definition of ethnographic fieldnotes "as the systematic ways of writing what one observes and learns while participating in the daily rounds of the lives of others" (Emerson, Fretz, and Shaw 1995). As the year progressed I fell into a system of sorts. I certainly recorded within the "lives of others." My journal served then as the fieldnotes of a teacher. Mine were records of headnotes (Emerson et al. 1995) and hard notes and heartnotes as well. The more I observed and made notes the more adept I became at documenting. Like learning scales and etudes builds the foundation for music, learning to record quickly and accurately built a foundation for my research. As I went back to flesh out the quickly written notes, filling in half written words and sentences, I often felt a keen connection to other stories (Connelly and Clandinin 1990) from my past. Those times I wrote long into the night or too long after school. That's when the memoirs surfaced. Writing them became a time when I allowed myself to listen to the wholeness of my life rather than just the present moment.

It felt a bit like stopping practice to play a piece of music I knew well enough to play with flair. When I played those pieces I shifted my attention from the notes on the page and connected with my cello almost physically. The bow slid across the strings with no effort, my fingers following commands from deep inside. Invariably I chastised myself for digressing. It felt "too good to be practice," I confessed to my teacher one day. "Oh no," she responded, "it is *essential* that you 'digress' everyday. It reminds you that there is sense to the scales, that they connect later to something larger *and* that there are compositions yet to be born!" At the end of the year, as I re-read the journal, I realized that the digressions formed parallel stories. Each story demanded to be interpreted in light of the other. I began to see the connectedness of the two stories. Each played a vital part in the composition that was born.

If we understand the "researcher as an instrument" (Emerson et al. 1995), it would behoove us to know that instrument and know it well, especially when the instrument is ourself. Writing memoirs while I documented the present helped me to know myself better and to understand my participants better as a result.

When I began to "chunk" the writing (LeCompte and Preissle 1993) into common themes in the memoirs, I could see them in context. I was able to connect some interactions between myself and the children that had triggered the memory. I began to understand how necessary it had been to hear the whole of my story as I documented the present one. Space limits what I am able to share, but I would like to write about two themes from the memoirs. They are representative of two large writing focuses, prejudice and family, and the leaping off spots for my biggest questions.

Andante: "Just Don't Talk About It"

When we were given our class lists I was surprised to have it attached to three very thick folders. Kindergarten teachers usually create permanent folders. We don't receive them. These children had double folders, which meant that at age four they were already receiving special education services. I knew I needed more than I had at my immediate disposal, materially or emotionally, to predict success for these already labeled children. During the first few weeks of school, family members of each of the children informed me that the children had a common problem. Each was a product of fetal alcohol syndrome (FAS) and/or crack cocaine exposure in utero.

Journal entry.

It has come to this, has it? Real live "crack babies" in my classroom! I had been waiting for this to happen in some place like New York City or maybe even Atlanta. I thought I would read about it. But I suppose the world stays quiet about the things that embarrass us and that we have no immediate answers for. It doesn't mean it's not happening, it doesn't mean that the subject is not being sensationalized on some TV magazine show. It just means we refuse to admit that the problem is commonplace and with us all the time. It means that we walk beside the problem every day, bumping shoulders with it and never turning to look it directly in the face. Something like elevator etiquette; face forward and don't talk.

We seventh grade girls were all in the school bathroom trying to comb our hair in the bit of mirror each could claim. Connie Woods, the leader of our group said, "Hannah makes me sick bragging about her baby brother all the time. You'd think that is the only thing she could talk about. Why can't she be like Karen?" (I don't know why she found favor with me today. Probably because I was in hearing distance, unlike poor Hannah.)

"Karen," she said turning to allow me another inch of mirror, "you don't ever talk about your baby sister. How old is she now?" I blushed beet red and answered, "Six months," hoping she would continue attacking some absent class member and stop asking me questions. There was nothing to say.

For Mother's entire pregnancy, I had talked of nothing else. The first month or two of my sister's life was the same way. But then I just stopped.

I was nearly thirteen when she was born. That fragile year when dolls are permanently stored in the attic. The year I found my skate key had rusted and childhood began to be past tense most of the time. I was NOT ready to leave it. A new baby sister felt like the granted wish of a fairy godmother. A live baby doll to play with and a reason to keep the toys and best loved books on the shelves and out of the attic.

But I wasn't prepared to know HER. I was in love with the idea of it all. She was beautiful. So perfectly formed on the outside. But the fairy godmother turned out to be the tricking kind . . . something was very wrong. This baby sister had seizures that were frightening. She rarely if ever made eye contact with me, and she never seemed any happier to be with us than with anyone else. But she could sit alone, pull up, and she crawled . . . right past us and the toys we waved in her path to get her attention.

"Well, why don't you talk about her?" My eyes were brimming with tears. I shrugged my shoulders. I hated Connie Woods and I hated Hannah Gallis and her baby brother, too. As the tears blurred my square inch of mirror, the bell rang. I couldn't wait for the next bell to ring, signaling dismissal, a way out . . . a solitary walk home. I love my baby sister. I do . . . really. Just don't talk about it. Just don't talk about it. It . . . my sister, the end of childhood for me and the beginning of a lifetime of childhood for her.

I saw the folders before I saw the children. But I had met the children when they were younger. I had taught each of their older siblings. But these siblings were different. They carried a tag and they were all in the same room—with *me*.

As I looked through Nat's folder, I remembered the first time I met him. He was about three years old the year I taught his sister. I went to visit the family in the home, and while I was there I met his mother. She was more like a sister, so young and so full of chatter and truly funny. Nat and the sister I was teaching were both cared for by the grandmother. She was letting the mother have the conference. We were almost unable to talk together because Nat was "all over the place." I asked the mother how old he was, but she couldn't remember. She hollered back to her mother, the custodial grandmother, who was staying in the background, "Mama, how old Nat is?" The grandmother was so embarrassed. She must have realized the cover was broken. I wondered how many times she had tried to deny the obvious. *Just don't talk about it. Just don't talk about it.*

I went to the other folders and had the same experiences of flashing back to visits with the families of Rodney and Loretta and seeing them as very small children. Their brothers and sisters were not without noticeable problems, and I began to reflect back on things I had observed in their behavior. I wondered about the time Loretta's brother had a huge scrape on his face and her mother called so worried that we would think she had hit him. "He is just clumsy," she said, "and that's why I wouldn't get him a bicycle so he go off on somebody else bike, and see he bust up his face!" I remembered his stoic personality coupled with his unpredictable outbursts, his perseveration on tasks and the inconsistency of performance almost minute by minute. Why wasn't I suspicious of something—or was I? *Just don't talk about it. Just don't talk about it.*

I looked at Rodney's huge folder of papers and felt grateful that he had received early intervention. His brother was much like Rodney. His face bore the marks of FAS. When his grandmother had come for conferences, I asked about the mother, whom I'd met only once (she had not been sober). "She's fine," his grandmother replied. Michael told me that he was living with "Mother" now, but the grandmother insisted that he was not. He claimed witness to domestic violence and repeated numerous anecdotes about his little brother Rodney, who at three years old, "couldn't talk but sure can cuss!" His grandmother shook her head and remarked quietly that Michael could "sure tell a tale." Cover. *Just don't talk about it.*

Reflecting further, and trying to understand, I began to see a bit of my *own* story in the memories of those encounters. I recognized my family in them. Not the drugs or the violence but the pride and the need to keep it ours alone. *Just don't talk about it. Just don't talk about it.*

The day I saw myself in the folders of those children, their labels became less indicting, less formidable. At the same time that their labels grew less important, their personhood grew more important and the tags they carried seemed to carry a higher price. The drive to get them comfortably contributing to the reading and writing "work" of our classroom community became paramount.

The day I saw my middle class white parents in the faces of these less afflu-ent black parents, I knew we had made some similar journeys. I recognized the unaddressed fear, I felt the cloak of words around explanations that would seem too raw if told point blank. I felt the accusal in their explanations and answers. "You wouldn't understand" was never spoken aloud but it bathed every phrase they uttered to me about their children. I did understand, but only in part. I had been the big sister, not the parent. I had been the big sister, not the child who constantly walked into failure and non-acceptance. And I was not black, never had been, never would be . . . Hold it! Don't talk about *that*! *Just don't talk about it.*

I know on reflection, and I think I knew then, that I was dealing with more than the obvious problem of the children's specific learning challenges. I was fac-ing the distance between our two cultures in a new way. Somewhere along the way I came to the realization that I could never fully understand their culture and their families until I understood my own. I couldn't embrace who they were until I was willing to embrace myself. That meant only one thing, I was going to have *to talk about it.*

The journal was the place I talked about it, at first safely and later more painfully.

Adagio: Reshaping to Teach

Here is the point where you may be asking, "What does all this memoir stuff have to do with teaching children to read and write? What does the past have to do with research?" I believe it has everything to do with teaching children to read and write when the memoirs remind a teacher at a value level that children approach writing and reading tasks with considerable variability (Dyson 1987). My memoirs helped me to know the difference between identifying reading and writing problems *in* my children and identifying my children *as* reading writing problems.

Each child faced a different set of challenges in the acquisition of reading. A common feature, however, was their inability to attend to the material presented to them. The coming together of the physical ability to attend, the emotional stamina to enter the material without hinderance, and the processing of my teaching hap-pened inconsistently and unpredictably. I had to learn to trust the natural desire to read that the children displayed. Recording memoirs of my sister Kathy learning to read, to spell, and count allowed me the patience to wait on the teachable moment, and then empowered me to capitalize on it without apology.

Rodney was not able to attend to a book at the beginning of school year. He wasn't really interested in holding and carrying books for a long time. And he hated to hear one read aloud. The act of sitting and listening seemed to cause him physical pain. I wondered if we would ever be able to read as a class without being distracted by his wanderings or by his rolling and moaning on the floor.

Remembering how Kathy hated the sound of a book-reading voice gave me patience. I watched Rodney begin to stop and watch us from a distance when we "sang" a book. At nap time one day he *requested* (causing considerable and prolonged disturbance) that I play the "meow-meow song." From those cues and from remembering Mother setting spelling words to music, I began to sing books to him. He was able to sit and listen and then say, "Do it again." He was hooked! I reshaped large group time to begin with a song. One of my teaching buddies loaned me a set of big books that were illustrated songs and we learned all of them. Eventually I forgot what brought Rodney to group. He and I grew accustomed to his presence in the group. The deliberate reshaping ebbed and flowed with other demands. Sometimes we didn't sing, but he was there for different reasons now.

Loretta wanted to hold and stack, in a seeming effort to possess the books. She also turned the pages and told her version of the story, very quietly in a whisper. She sat in the reading corner with a "baby doll" in her lap and looked at the pages of books intently. If someone else came to the reading corner, she left carrying the stack of books and the baby doll with her to another spot in the room. It wasn't always like that. I remembered the first week of school when she stood in the middle of the room refusing to make contact with me or with other children during center and small group time. At large group time, however, she was mesmerized by the story. Later in the week she went to the home living center alone and rocked the baby until some other children came over. Then she took her spot in the middle of the floor again, staring at nothing and daring me to make her move.

I have always thought that rules about centers were important in kindergarten, especially the ones about things staying where they belong. I expected that the books stay in the book corner, the dolls in the house, and the blocks with the blocks. It makes sense that way, and it teaches order. One day I recorded in my journal how Kathy had challenged a long-standing family rule and reshaped our week ends.

In my strict southern Baptist upbringing we kept the Sabbath holy in many ways. One of them was my parents' refusal to engage in paid-for entertainment on Sunday. That meant no swimming, no movies, no golf, etc. Now, Kathy was a precocious swimmer, mastering the water early. It was wonderful to see her jumping off the diving board when she was two or three years old. There she excelled. She knew it was hot and she knew it was afternoon and time to swim. She could make no sense of the Sunday rule. She was miserable, and that meant we were going to be miserable, too. The No Swimming on Sunday rule was dropped (not easily and not quickly) and the whole family benefitted from reshaping the notion of honoring-the-day by celebrating together Kathy's gift.

Loretta challenged the rule about where the doll baby stayed and where the books stayed. I could fight the rules or I could celebrate the way she read to her baby doll so that I could hear how she read the books she had heard in large group. I could challenge the rule about the books staying in the book corner or I could be glad that I didn't have to give her special center time. The whole class benefitted from the reshaping of the rules. Children began to create new places to read and to write. The books began to wander to mats at nap time and to places to be "copied" for their own books. I took their lead and brought big baskets to hold books. The book corner soon became only one place where books could be read. They were all over the room now.

Nat was unable at first to attend in large group but he connected in a small group or with an individual reading to him. He was most drawn to books with "props." On the special days that I had something to use to help re-tell the story, he went straight to that place loudly re-telling the stories. One day my mother dropped by after school. She saw the masks beside the copy of *The Little Red Hen*. She remarked that she wished Kathy had been exposed to some of the things she saw happening in my room. Over twenty years later she still has the leftover dream that Kathy could have been taught in a setting where she really belonged. That night in my journal I didn't write how Kathy had helped me to reach Nat, but instead how Nat had helped me reach an understanding about Kathy.

The oldest questions about Kathy, even the unanswerable one (Why?), were feeding the immediacy of my questions. Although I had recorded many connections based on lessons with Kathy, it was actually the fact that so much *didn't* work that kept me open to shaping and reshaping the materials of my craft.

I have felt responsible for Kathy all her life. I have had the nauseating experience of having people tell us what we "ought" to do. It sounds like blame. Writing about that exposed nerve feeling helped me to dwell on what *I* could do for Rodney, Nat and Loretta instead of blaming their birth circumstances. Recording stories of people who gave up on Kathy because she was difficult caused me to reexamine what I really expected from my special students.

Largo: Facing My Prejudices

When a child comes to me pre-labeled and double-foldered and stamped "lower socio-economic, African-American," how does that affect my expectations for that child? I began asking myself tough questions when I felt accused of my whiteness. I was uncomfortable talking to an African-American teaching assistant at times because I was so carefully trying not to offend him. I wanted to ask questions but I was always very careful to practice not seeing color. I wanted to ask what he meant at times, but didn't know how to ask, to admit I noticed. I wished I was able to so freely talk to the African-American parents like he did. Writing memories of the earliest encounters with people who were not "like me" caused me to look hard at my unexamined assumptions about blackness.

Reading Lisa Delpit's *Other People's Children* continues to present me with the accusation that African-American teachers have felt left out of the discourse on reading education. I saw myself there. Red-faced, sweaty-palmed, I had to admit being a part of that "new prejudice." The words are different but the messages enter the same data bank, leaving African-American children in a "less than" place. I tried to deny it; but through honest writing I acknowledged what I thought did not, could not, exist.

The questions recorded in my journal record some of the painful self-interrogation: How can you teach someone you don't expect to learn? How do you seriously hand a child a piece of paper and tell him to write when you see a less-than-able child before you? How do you talk and partner with parents when you feel so sorry for their plight that you just gloss over the child's struggles in order to keep them from knowing what they already know? How do you teach a child that you have fallen in love with differently from one that you haven't? How do you hold your own sister's hand through a lesson differently than you hold another child's?

Journal entry.

I guess I always felt, being a child of the 60s, that if I sang the Coca-Cola commercial long enough I would be an unbiased teacher.
"I'd like to teach the world . . . ."
Hadn't I survived being called "nigger-lover" in high school?
"To sing in perfect harmony . . ."
Didn't I truly believe that all are created equal?
"I'd like to buy the world a home . . ."
Didn't I say over and over, "all people are the same only their color is different."?
"And furnish it with love . . ."
I mean, once I was going to be a missionary—to AFRICA! Now aren't they black there?
"Buy apple trees and honey bees and snow white turtle doves . . ."
Who would dare suggest that I should examine my feelings about race?
"It's the real thing . . . what the world wants today . . ."
We were standing in front of a large mirror playing dress-up at Kay's house.

As we changed from one gaudy outfit after another to try to transform our five-year-old bodies into something that resembled a starlet, we saw our overly made-up faces in stark contrast to our bare white chests marked only by suntan lines and two brown nipples. In my very southern accent I asked her, "Do colored[2] children have brown ninnies or white ones?"

"Don't have neither one," she responded, " 'cause they don't make colored children."

"They most certainly do," I said. "Where do you think the grown–up ones come from?"

"Did you ever see a colored child?"

"No-o-o . . . don't guess so."

There was the sound of the noon whistle, which meant that Daddies all over the little southern town would soon be home for lunch—'scuse me, *dinner*. We ate dinner in the middle of the day, supper at night. (Yankees ate lunch.) Kay and I scurried to get the make-up off and put our clothes back on because as soon as her Daddy walked in, he would call us and my favorite time of visiting Kay would come. Feeding the prisoners!

You see Kay lived at the jail. Her Daddy was the sheriff. Her great tall house was half jail and half residence of the sheriff. The court house was next door and the church right across the alley. Feeding the prisoners was the way we knew what we were going to have to eat that day because we ate the same great food as the prisoners, prepared not by Kay's mother but by cooks. Fried chicken, pork chops, macaroni pie, chocolate pudding, cat-head biscuits, garden fresh tomatoes, and corn. Um-um. The cooks were black women who were called trustees. Sort of quasi-prisoners, gentle as lambs and dressed in green uniforms. The "nurse" (baby sitter) was also one of

---

2. The use of "colored" situates this event in time and region.

these black trustees, as was the gardener and the yard man and a number of others, as I remember. Kay and I were allowed to go into the jail, which was through a swinging door on the other side of the kitchen from the entrance to her dining room, where we would eat. We delivered the plates and chatted with the prisoners, who were all black and all very nice to us. The doors were not locked and the men were sitting on their beds playing cards or talking. This particular day I noticed a man sleeping in a cell toward the back. The Sheriff told us to leave him alone. "He's not ready to wake up yet. He'll eat later."

"But he's white," I whispered.

"You'll never guess what is down in that jail, Daddy," I said that night. "A white man. In jail!! Why are those people in jail, Daddy?"

Where were the "colored" children? Why didn't we see one another, and why were the only colored people I ever saw prisoners? And if prisoners were bad people, what were they doing walking around out of the jail? Was the cook or the woman who watched us out in the yard once bad but now good? Or did they wind up in jail by mistake? Would they rather take care of little colored children than us?

Sometime later we began to get "Little Rascals" on TV. I had confirmation.

There were colored children. Maybe not here, but they were in television land. "I wish I had me a little colored boy or girl to play with." I ventured to my own baby sitter one rainy sit-inside day. "The very idea!! Don't be nasty." The look of shock and disapproval said it all, or at least more than I would undo in the next forty years.

What does it mean to be prejudiced? How does it shape us as teachers of children from another culture? Could I be operating through messages I logged in early in my life? Does prejudice inform the way I address these children? Each of them has a parent currently serving a jail sentence. Each of them lives in what John Ogbu (1977) calls a "caste-like" minority, vested with little hope of walking out of it. Each of us by social design and personal choices are celled off from truly knowing each other's culture. Prisons can be self–made, I've come to understand.

It is possible that I viewed the ability to read and write in a kind of prisoner-jailer metaphor, as if freedom and power came from the level of literacy a child had reached. If so, was that a positive framework for presenting the school brand of reading and writing, or a negative framework? It is my job to make available the power of the written word to all children. It is my job to scrutinize the ideology of my white-female-southern-middle-class upbringing to address ways I may stand in the way of the equal dissemination of that power? From the time I learned that "colored children" existed and were brown underneath their shirts, I adamantly denounced a prejudice in myself. Skin pigmentation had been addressed in my life and I was done with it. Oh so painfully I know that ethnocentrism is a part of my life. I made new progress through the writing and I came away from the year determined to read as many voices in the African-American writing community and history as I could.

Accepting my previously unexamined attitudes was an important step in teaching Rodney, Loretta, and Nat. Was I just "playing with" them? Was I just in love with the idea? Was I ready to accept them for all they were now and not for the past that had labeled them crack babies? Accepting the answers to some of those questions was a necessary step in recognizing their parents as co-teachers, partners in the education of their children.

Journal entry.

> I had to walk out of my missionary mentality to become a questioning educator. I have addressed children as parts of my job, as pets, as vessels to be filled, as products, and as the little bearers of news from the classroom that would build my reputation in the eyes of their parents. When their parents were prestigious it mattered more. It hurts me to write those words.

When I began seriously listening to my life, my teaching life, I began to listen to my students' lives at a different level. When I looked behind the picture the public saw of my family, I became more tolerant of those who were different from me. When I began to stop and examine the flashes of memory that jolted me, I became a more patient teacher. I more often saw the students and their parents as people; people walking in and out of pain, in and out of joy, in and out of socially constructed prisons.

I saw myself, the teacher, walking in and out of the same pain and joy, and in and out of the same socially constructed alienation. In a way I *was* still feeding the prisoners. I took my ethnocentrism and smilingly dished up my expectations. As they cleaned their plates I wonder that I never noticed they might need seconds.

Andantino: Examining Choices and Expectations

Expectations. When I looked full into the face of my mill-village roots and compared the indictment from the town people against my parents during their childhood, I wanted to make sure I checked social indictment in my assessment of children. "Mill children don't need a good school. After all, they were bred to work the mill. Bunch of lint–heads can't learn much beyond the basics."

My father failed the fifth grade and barely squeaked by some of the others. Those teachers didn't expect much of him and he didn't give them much. His Ph.D is all the sweeter now, but how many others believed the messages they were sent?

Journal entry.

> I was standing in front of the mirror in my parents' bedroom while Mother fixed my hair. It was Sunday and of course we would be going to Mama and Grandaddy's house after church. I thought about Grandaddy.
>
> "How does Grandaddy tie his shoe without his hand?"
>
> "Oh he can do anything. I've never known him with his hand; he lost it when a young boy working in the mill."
>
> "Lost it?"
>
> "It got cut real bad in a big machine when he was working."
>
> "Then what happened?"
>
> "He had to have it amputated and so the mill offered him a college education or two thousand dollars. He took the money because they needed it so bad. See, he couldn't work until his hand healed, so they needed the money."
>
> "Did he do right? Did he take the right thing?"
>
> "Well . . . I don't think he did, but I was not there. I don't know everything."

And the faraway look was there. The unspoken story about Grandaddy. The words that would stop on occasion when I entered the room. Sh-h-h. *Just don't talk about it.*

Everybody in our very large family knew that Grandaddy had a drinking problem except me and my siblings. I didn't know until I was an adult. But I knew something was wrong. I could feel it. Low expectations of one who had big dreams. Money constraints that were so big and so socially unalterable that the choice was really not a choice. The money couldn't bring his arm back, and it couldn't bring his twin brothers back either. They were much younger, in fact, just infants, when he was a young adult. He came home from work one day and found that his mother had allowed them to be adopted. *Just don't talk about it.* He died in his seventies and the twins had not been mentioned in over fifty years. He wouldn't allow it. *Just don't talk about it.*

Well, times were different, I've been told. For who? What do "the times" have to do with poverty? What do "the times" have to do with uninformed choices?

Alcohol was a way out for my Granddaddy. Alcohol and crack were a way out for the parents of these children. Stupid choices? Looking for quick money and quick fixes? Surely they realize the fallacy of that thinking. Don't they realize what they've done to their children? All of those questions deserve thought, but the people don't deserve condemnation. The bottom line is that I have children to teach who will never be able to walk away from the past. I have a grandfather who was never free from the haunting physical reminder of the kind of poverty that allowed children to become maimed and separated from families.

When I looked at the physical deformities in Rodney's hands and feet, I thought of Grandaddy. With fused wrists and shortened fingers, Rodney learned to cut with scissors and paint and write and become the best builder in our community of learners. You see, if Grandaddy could do it with one hand, I was sure Rodney could do it with two, however limited they were. Expectations—high ones informed from memoir and the stories in my life.

When I practice the details in a repetitive cello line, I "hear" more than those oom-pahs, I hear the whole of the orchestra. Holding the total score gives the practice of my single line a context and meaning. Holding the memory of Kathy, Grandaddy, the mill village, the whole of my living, gave context and meaning as I observed and recorded the details of this year's story. People who hear an individual practice can hear only the boom-ba-boom-ba-boom. It takes hearing the collection of individual instruments all playing at once, carefully synchronized and interpreted, to make a symphony. My aim in writing this piece has been to come to symphony out of the carefully synchronized and interpreted journaling of individual stories of the present and the past.

References

Beuchner, F. 1991. *Telling Secrets.* San Francisco: HarperCollins.

Beuchner, F. 1992. *Clown in the Belfry.* San Francisco: HarperCollins.

Calkins, L. 1991. *Living Between the Lines.* Portsmouth, NH: Heinemann.

Connelly, F. and J. Clandinin. 1990. "Stories of Experience and Narrative Inquiry." *Educational Review* 19(5): 2–14.

Delpit, L. 1995. *Other People's Children.* New York: New York Press.

Dyson, A. 1987. "Individual Differences in Beginning Composing." *Written Communication* 4(4): 411–442.

Emerson, R., R. Fretz, and L. Shaw. 1995. *Writing Ethnographic Fieldnotes.* Chicago: University of Chicago Press.

Gornick, V. 1996. "The Memoir Boom." *Women's Review of Books* XIII: 1–5.

Greene, M. 1985. "A Philosophic Look at Merit and Mastery in Teaching." *The Elementary School Journal* 86: 17–26.

LeCompte, M. and J. Preissle. 1993. *Ethnography and Qualitative Design in Educational Research* (second edition). San Diego: Academic Press.

Ogbu, J. 1977. *Minority Education and Caste.* New York: Academic Press.

THREE

Ownership and the Well-Planned Study

Ann Keffer, Debby Wood, Shelley Carr, Leah Mattison, and Barbara Lanier

Comer Elementary School

**W**ho decides what teacher research is and how it is to be conducted? Whose place is it to say what constitutes a valid method of data collection and analysis for teachers examining their own practice in their own classrooms? Who owns the questions, the timeline, the design? Who owns teacher research?

Before our membership in the School Research Consortium, we—five classroom teachers from Comer Elementary School in rural Georgia—could have neither answered nor even asked those questions. Having heard them asked, we would have assumed that if we waited patiently, someone in a position of higher authority would tell us the answers. Only gradually, during our three years as teacher researchers, have we come to realize the importance of answering them for ourselves. Our experiences have led us to believe that to allow anyone other than teacher researchers to define teacher research is to relinquish the opportunity to make our own meanings from the research we pursue.

When we signed up to be part of the SRC and investigate "our most burning questions concerning literacy learning," we thought that by becoming a community of writers ourselves we could in the first year examine the evolution of our community and our growth as adult writers, and then in the second year document how our new identities as "real" writers changed the way we taught writing. One of our crucial concerns was to become better writing teachers. We thought we had found a way to move toward that goal while at the same time investigating the dynamics of membership in a community of learners. We therefore formulated the research question: How does membership in a community of writers affect our perceptions of ourselves as writers and as teachers of writing? We had a well-planned, two-year study.

For the first five months of the first year, we held biweekly, two-hour meetings at school. A typical meeting consisted of one or more members reading aloud their personal writing and/or describing their writing experiences; other members responding with encouragement, praise, criticism, advice, or experiences of their own; and the group as a whole attempting to generalize about its experiences and to assess the status of the project. We collected data consisting of participants' personal writing, including journal entries, and audiotapes of group meetings. The audiotapes were transcribed for data analysis and returned to research group members as quickly as possible.

In January, having accumulated five months' worth of data and feeling a bit frantic, we scheduled the first of three bimonthly day-long retreats away from school. During the morning portion of these retreats we focused on data analysis; the afternoons were given to sharing and discussing our writing. To compensate for less frequent group meetings, we assigned ourselves "writing buddies" with whom to meet frequently to continue to support each other as writers.

Each of us arrived at the three bi-monthly meetings having read through selected transcripts and highlighted portions she considered important. At the meetings, we divided into pairs for the purpose of comparing highlighted material, looking for meaningful topics of talk that appeared frequently and/or extended across multiple transcripts. The pairs then brought their quotes and tentative topic lists back to the whole group where, by sharing and discussing what we had found in our pairs, we realized the topics could be organized around three broad themes: what we learned about being teacher researchers, what we learned about the dynamics of community, and what we discovered about writing.

Having brought order to our data, we were ready to write. By the end of the summer we had produced an article detailing our first year's experiences, which was subsequently published in *Language Arts* (Keffer et al. 1994).

According to our research design, our second year we were supposed to find out how our experiences as writers changed our teaching, the strong presumption being that we would have improved. We felt intuitively that there must be an advantage inherent in having done some of the things we were trying to get our students to do. Yet as soon as we set our minds to determining just how we would gather data to investigate our assumptions, we were overcome by a lassitude, a resistance so strong that we couldn't seem to force ourselves to focus on the problem. We canceled meetings and made excuses. We avoided each other in the halls. We planned procedures and didn't carry them out. At this point, we later disclosed, each of us secretly questioned the efficacy of trying to teach and carry out a research project simultaneously.

Finally, in an attempt to regain the energy of our first year, we tinkered with our research question. In our adult writers' workshop, we had discussed at length the relationship between the genres we read and the genres we most wanted to write. We hypothesized that the reason some of us didn't place a high value on our own personal narrative was that it wasn't a genre we often read. Our students too read mostly fiction. Perhaps if we exposed them to quality personal narrative they could be inspired to value more highly writing from their own lives. Instead of our original question, "How does membership in a community of writers affect our perceptions of ourselves as teachers of writing?" we settled on, "To what extent and in what ways will our deliberate exposure of our students to high-quality personal narrative affect their enthusiasm for writing it?"

We designed surveys to measure our students' desire to write personal narrative as compared with their interest in other genres. We administered the surveys before and after a three-week period during which we read aloud daily examples of writing from real life: picture books like *The Hating Book* by Charlotte Zolotow (1969), short chapter books like *The Big Lie* by Isabella Leitner (1992), stories based heavily on remembered events like Ann's own "Bullfrogs for Breakfast," essays like those in Roald Dahl's *Boy* (1984), and poems like "Oranges" by Gary Soto (1988). The surveys showed little if any change in the students' attitudes toward personal narrative writing, and the sample writings we required from them showed little if any improvement.

At that point, feeling that our best teaching efforts had a negligible effect on our students, each of us sat down with her own students around a tape recorder and picked their brains. Other than being pleased that the children took our questions seriously and that they gave us a few fresh reasons for their reluctance to write from their lives, we found nothing positive in these interviews. It took us the better part of a year to dig down deep enough to find the significance of what we had done and what our students had told us. It took us even longer to realize that embedded in what we perceived as our failure was a more crucial lesson that bore on the degree of willingness, enthusiasm, and purpose we brought to our research. In our first year, we felt ownership; in our second year we did not.

We owned our research when *we had an authentic question.*

Of course we stated it more formally, but in our heads our first year's question was, "What would it be like to be in a writing workshop and try our hands at being writers?" We couldn't wait to find out. We, like many adults, had often entertained an ambition to write. More than that, we suspected that the experience we were engineering for ourselves would provide valuable insights into how our students experienced the learning environment we provided for them. Our question was of genuine and immediate concern to us as teachers and relevant to our individual classrooms, arising as it did out of our school's transition to whole language instruction in language arts. Our enthusiasm for the entire research project started with our belief in the importance of the question.

Why, then, when the time came that we had said—in our well-planned study—that we would investigate the transfer of what we'd learned as adult writers to teaching young writers couldn't we capture the same enthusiasm? First, we hadn't had sufficient time to absorb the changes brought about by the first year's research. In a little over a year's time we had become members of the SRC, tackled a research project, written a paper that was in press at the NRRC and under consideration by a national educational journal, and made presentations at local, state, and national conferences, all for the first time. We needed time to bask in our accomplishments and get used to our new identities.

Second, we realized that although we had spent a year as members of an adult writing workshop, had produced quite a bit of writing, and certainly knew more about writing than we did initially, we hadn't allowed ourselves enough time to develop as writers to the point that we felt expert enough to tackle the second part of our question. We felt confident that the writing workshops we conducted in our classrooms would be different because of our experiences, but we knew it would not be as if professional writers had taken over our classes.

Third, several of us had undergone professional or personal changes that caused us to develop new, more pertinent, more "burning questions" to explore through research. Instead of feeling obligated to continue our well-planned study, we should have looked more honestly at our changed situations and let new research foci evolve from them. Instead, we let the commitment we felt toward a question we had fashioned two years previously draw us down a path we were no longer inspired to travel.

We owned our research when *we controlled its design.*

Probably our most serious mistake as novice teacher researchers was to commit ourselves to a two-year research design before we had any experience at research. We stuck doggedly to the two-year design even when it wasn't working because we thought we had to. We didn't realize that a written design is seldom the lived design of classroom research. More experienced teacher researchers might have cautioned us to be prepared to adjust our plan, to speed it up, slow it down, change its emphasis, or abandon it midstream.

Another stumbling block that came from our inexperience was assuming that we had to incorporate traditional teacher-research methodology. Instead of helping, methods like keeping teaching journals or trying to videotape our classes or trying to take notes and teach at the same time just made the process more difficult for us. We eventually found that, during our first year, the "talk" that was occurring at every meeting was our best data. We just needed to preserve it so we could later analyze it. The transcriptions of these meetings led us to the discovery of meaning in our research.

During the second year, too often we felt we were forcing ourselves and our students to do things that weren't a natural part of our classroom. Knowing that we would be reporting our study led us to focus more on methods that would result in data that was easy to analyze and write about. What we should have done was to recognize data that was already available to us, such as children's writing portfolios, and structures that were already in place, like grade level meetings. By using these organic methods, we could have made research a part of our teaching instead of a tacked-on burden.

After two years, we know that classroom research is not something a teacher does in her "spare time." Research should shape itself to the natural rhythms of the school year. Like any other part of teaching, the intensity with which we pursue it will ebb and flow to accommodate other demands on us and our students. Ideally, classroom research becomes an indispensable part of an approach to teaching in which theory informs practice and practice informs theory continually and immediately right in the classroom. As important as it is to ask ourselves what questions we most want to answer through our research, it is just as important to ask ourselves what questions most need to be answered to benefit a particular group of children, and what questions they are peculiarly suited to help us answer.

We owned our research when *we claimed our own place in the research community.*

University researchers and teacher researchers have common goals: Finding better ways to educate children. Each can do so from his/her unique position and in the ways that best suit that position, thus complementing rather than duplicating each other's efforts. It was essential for us to find our own place in the research community, distinct from the university researcher.

The educational research with which we were most familiar (largely from our education courses) was conducted by university researchers from a positivist perspective, dividing children into experimental and control groups, applying treatments, and collecting hard data to subject to statistical analysis. Initially, we assumed that we were to do the same. In our *Language Arts* article, we described our discomfort with the prospect. "We imagined all research to be a tangle of experimental and control groups, double-tailed t-tests, and analyses of variance. We doubted our competence and questioned our willingness to commit ourselves to the effort we knew such a project would require" (Keffer, Carr, Lanier, Mattison, Wood, and Stanulis 1996, 113). Our NRRC coordinators helped us to understand the difference between qualitative and quantitative research; but even so, months into our project our transcripts show us wondering, "I still want to know, where's the treatment? Where are the data?" "How are we going to know anything really happened? Won't we have just a bunch of anecdotal material when we get through?"

Eventually, we realized that we only made ourselves unhappy when we tried to force our research into a mold that didn't suit our situations as teachers or our modes of thought, conditioned by decades in the classroom. This is not to say that teachers cannot conduct quantitative research if we want to, but only to suggest that teachers should take care to preserve our unique perspective while doing whatever kind of research we choose.

During our first year of research, Debbie was part of a presentation at a national conference. One of the other participants, a university researcher, challenged Debbie's position that teacher stories are an important part of teacher research, saying something to the effect that if you can't show a change in student behavior, it is not really research. This anecdote serves to illustrate the kind of pressure teacher researchers may come under from those committed to the traditional university researcher perspective. While we and other teachers at the conference found value in the idea of teachers forming their own writing workshop, this person attacked our plan as worthless because we were not immediately applying a treatment to a group of children. Teachers can choose to study ourselves and our own practice without regard to anyone else's notion of what teacher research should be. While teachers seldom have the luxury of flexible schedules and outside funding, neither do our jobs depend on publishing. Without the pressure to publish, and whenever possible without the control of outside agencies, teachers are free to find new ways to conduct and share our research, ways that can also become a normal part of our growth as professionals. Some years we may have the time to approach those questions that we "wonder" about. Other years we may find that "worry about" conditions in our classrooms take precedence. Each of the individual circumstances we encounter can help us establish ownership of our place in the larger research community.

We owned our research when *our research community worked for us, not against us.*

Embarking on teacher research for the first time can be scary, and knowing there are others going through the process is comforting. It was motivating to share a common purpose. The group not only provided abundant positive reinforcement, but also served to legitimize its members' efforts. It was beneficial to find support from others when we hit hurdles and had to make critical decisions. Membership in a research team allowed us to capitalize on each others' strengths and work around individual shortcomings. Different group members were able to provide humor, nurturing, organization, leadership, inspiration, and food at different times as needed. One member or another was almost always able to rejuvenate us when our energy flagged.

At the same time that we were experiencing the effects of membership in our community of writers, we were also experiencing the effects of membership in a larger community, the community composed of the NRRC coordinators and all the teacher researchers within the SRC. Though it met only a few times during the year, this larger community affected us powerfully. Under its influence, we found ourselves engaging in behaviors we had not previously considered, such as making presentations at state and international reading conferences and preparing manuscripts for submission to professional journals. Teaching can be an isolated profession, especially teaching in a small, rural school. Association with other professionals, we found, energized us and renewed our pride in our roles as professional educators.

As much as it lends support and encouragement, there is a danger that the group can usurp the ownership of individual goals and questions. Between the first and second year, members of our group underwent changes that placed new demands on time and attention as well as created new research interests. Shelley switched from teaching a hard-of-hearing class to teaching a self-contained third grade class that contained one of her students. She became interested in studying the differences in teaching a hard-of-hearing child in a mainstream situation instead of on an individual basis.

Debbie had taught kindergarten, then served in a teacher resource position during the transition to whole language in her school. When she began teaching third grade, she was constantly planning themes, learning again how to interact with parents and grade-level peers, and making what seemed like millions of decisions. She might have studied the contrast between helping others become whole language teachers and applying whole language in her own classroom, at a new grade level.

A student transferred from another school that Ann wanted and needed to understand better. He had a brilliant mind—and Tourette's Syndrome. He alienated both students and teachers with his verbal outbursts and sometimes physical aggression. Slowly that year he used his exceptional intellect, with support from

Ann, to manage his problematic behaviors. Ann regretted at the end of the year that she had not studied how a real outsider can become a member of a classroom community.

Leah entered a master's program while still teaching full time and during the year lost both parents within a day of each other to heart attacks. Barbara endured a divorce and learned how to be both full-time single parent full-time teacher. Under these stressful circumstances, these researchers needed a leave of absence.

All of us might have been happier during our second year of research if we had taken the steps that our changed personal and professional lives suggested to us instead of feeling bound to our original research proposal. In retrospect, we realize that we could have maintained our close association as a study group with a focus on supporting each others' future research efforts.

We owned our research when *we were brutally honest.*

It was easy to be honest during our first year of research. No one really expected anything from us. We felt no guilt; we didn't worry about disappointing anyone. The second year, we had a reputation to live up to. The research on our adult writing community had been well received at conferences and had been accepted for publication. While others in the SRC struggled, we seemed successful. The prospect of failure might have caused dissembling on a level that we couldn't recognize at the time. At first we didn't recognize the fear—fear of embarrassment as teachers (What if I'm not good at teaching writing and someone finds out?) and as researchers (What if we can't do the project we planned? What if we can't collect data, or if the students don't grow as writers? What if the study gets no respect?). We should have trusted our knowledge, saying along with Sylvia Ashton-Warner, "I know because I was there."

We should have admitted to each other and NRRC our doubts and fears as well as our desire to abandon (at least temporarily) our original plan. We should have jumped up and down and shouted at each other, if necessary, instead of politely avoiding each other and SRC director Betty out of guilt. We wasted a lot of time making excuses for cutting our project down to manageable size. We had to own our failure before we could learn from it.

We write this chapter in the summer, and to be honest, we don't know exactly what our research questions will be in the coming year. That is not to say we don't have research plans, just that we now know those plans can and in some cases must change once we have begun the teaching/learning dialogue with a new group of students. Ann has become increasingly concerned about standardized testing, and "wants to have something to say" as a researcher about how it drives the curriculum. Leah's inquiry might be a little closer to home; she is a new mother. Barbara is most drawn in by being a member of the team; she may collaborate with another teacher or design her own study. Debby and Shelley will be team teaching in third grade; they want to study the process of creative grouping, individual conferences, and activity centers. Some aspect of these plans may become the focus of our inquiry; or something we could not possibly have anticipated—a child, an opportunity, a problem—may dictate our direction. Planning research is not something teachers do two years in advance. It is something we do continuously.

To answer the questions we raised at the beginning of this chapter: We as teacher researchers decide: It's our place only when we make it our place, and we have to work at owning the research. Taking that responsibility may be painful at times. But in order to own teacher research we have to be honest with our ourselves, our question, our design, our community, and our place in the larger research picture. We approach this honesty by keeping our commitment to improving our practice, to our students, and to each other. We talk, we teach, we write, we question. And we will not plan future studies without knowing our classrooms, our students, and ourselves.

References

Ashton-Warner, S. 1963. *Teacher.* New York: Simon & Schuster.

Dahl, R. 1984. *Boy: Tales of Childhood.* New York: Farrar, Straus and Giroux.

Leitner, I. 1992. *The Big Lie: A True Story.* New York: Scholastic.

Keffer, A. 1994. "Bullfrogs for Breakfast." Unpublished short story.

Keffer, A., S. Carr, B. Lanier, L. Mattison, D. Wood, and R. Stanulis. 1994. "Teacher Researchers Discover Magic in Forming an Adult Writing Workshop." *Language Arts* 73(2): 113–121.

Soto, G. 1988. "Oranges." In *The Music of What Happens: Poems That Tell Stories,* ed. P. Janeczko, 25-26. New York: Orchard.

Zolotow, C. 1969. *The Hating Book.* New York: HarperCollins.

FOUR

Keeping Students at the Center of Teacher Research

Georgiana Sumner, Johni Mathis, and Michelle Commeyras

We sat silently looking at each other. The realities of our students' lives overwhelmed us. We wanted to motivate our elementary and middle school students through literacy partnerships, but were these partnerships helping or harming our students? We are Johni and Georgiana, and we are sisters and teachers. Our concern came about during the second year we partnered students across our classes of racially and economically diverse eighth graders (Johni's students) and second graders (Georgiana's students). Michelle, a university teacher, provided support and counsel during our teacher researcher journey. In this chapter we draw upon our two years of research to explain the ways in which we have learned to keep students at the center of teacher research. We realized over the course of two years of studying literacy partnerships that our questions had to change if we wanted to keep the children's needs and best interests central to the research. We agree that it is important to begin with some preliminary questions. For example, we began studying whether the literacy partnerships were motivating students and how they were motivating them. However, during the second year, as we began to know more about the students, our central question changed.

Literacy Partnerships

We began that second year excited about the successful literacy partnerships that our students had experienced the previous year. Our goal was to study a new year of partnerships between second and eighth graders that incorporated ideas and suggestions that students from the first year gave us during class meetings and interviews. In general we expected the literacy partnerships to function much as they had during the previous year; thus, we began that second year with confidence. However, something was different. There seemed to be more at stake this year than just educational concerns. Questions arose that involved the emotional well-being of our students. Were the partnerships supportive? Our increased awareness of the turmoil in our students' lives weighed heavily on our minds. It was understandable that students might feel alienated from school work because many were suffering emotionally: A mother with breast cancer, a student in jail, a student pregnant, a molested child, a father murdered, and many home situations in transition. The lives of our second- and eighth-grade students brought new meaning to the statistics we read about children in the United States. According to Marian Wright Edelman, president of the Children's Defense Fund,

> Every 9 seconds a child drops out of school, every 14 seconds a child is arrested, every 15 minutes a baby dies, every 2 hours a child is killed by a firearm, every 4 hours a child commits suicide, every 7 hours a child dies from abuse or neglect. (Herbert 1996, 21)

We needed to know what the partnerships would do to or for these fragile lives. This became the focus of our second year of studying literacy partnerships. We explain how we have learned to do teacher research that keeps student interests at the center with examples from our two years of studying cross-age literacy partnerships. We begin with some background information on the literacy partnership project.

We created cross-age partnerships because we wanted to find new ways of motivating students for literacy. The centerpiece of the literacy partnerships has been that each class (second and eighth grade) discusses the same selections of children's literature (e.g., *The Black Snowman, Jumanji*). Other elements that the students chose to add to the partnership have included exchanging autobiographies between partners, writing letters to partners about the literature discussions, and reading student-authored books. Most important to the children each year were the times when the two classes met to read and visit together. At the end of the first year we wrote about how the interpersonal relationships that developed between partners generated intrinsic motivation for literate activity (Commeyras, Mathis, and Sumner 1995).

Students' Decisions Yield Data

> It would be nice if they [the administration] agreed on what you have got to teach [but] how you teach it is up to you. Then you could have students involved. (Georgiana, Research Meeting on May 15, 1995)

Each year of research began with a proposal outlining research questions and some general procedures with the caveat that there would be ongoing participation from the students in defining the elements of the partnerships. The students' decisions about aspects of the partnerships yielded a variety of sources of data. In the first year after the eighth graders were paired with second graders, Johni began discussions about how to proceed in setting up the project. The students decided to introduce themselves by writing autobiographies for their partners. After hearing that the eighth graders were writing autobiographies, Georgiana's second graders enthusiastically voted to write their own autobiographies.

By involving students in making decisions about what would occur between literacy partners, we were creating a research context whereby new sources of data were created by students. The decision to write autobiographies was data in that it told us that students felt it was important to share personal information as a means of launching the partnerships. Furthermore, reading the autobiographies as data gave us important insights into the lives and aspirations of the students that we might not have otherwise known. One example from the second year of partnerships that we find particularly significant comes from the autobiography that eighth grader Samuel wrote for Tyler, his second-grade partner.

> I love to have fun with my friends . . . but we always get our work done in class. In the future I would like to become a police officer. If I become a police officer I can change everything I have done bad. (Excerpted from Samuel's autobiography)

Samuel had come to Johni's class from the Youth Detention Center and was still on probation. What Samuel thought important to tell Tyler was particularly significant to Johni because it allowed her to see how Samuel felt about what had been happening in his life. It was also helpful to both Johni and Georgiana because they were concerned about partnering Samuel with Tyler. Tyler was having difficulty adapting to a new school, making friends, and feeling successful academically. Georgiana had learned that Tyler's sister was schizophrenic, which was having a dramatic effect on Tyler's home life. He often had emotional outbursts at school lasting 30 to 45 minutes. It seemed of utmost importance that Tyler have a supportive literacy partner. The contents of Samuel's autobiography provided some reassurance to Georgiana and Johni that Samuel might be a good literacy partner for Tyler.

The autobiographies were an important source of data that were not part of our original plan. We now understand that data sources in teacher research may be realized along the way rather than always being predetermined as in experimental research designs. What remains a challenge is to recognize what might be useful as data. We find that continually reviewing either your original or emerging questions should guide you in identifying what kind of data is needed or available given what students are doing as school work. The idea that what needs to be viewed as data becomes evident during the research has been acknowledged by qualitative researchers.

> Choosing issues helps us define data sources and data-gathering activities. We are likely to make observations, to interview to get observations of things we cannot see ourselves, and to review documents. Doing these things will usually cause us to reconsider our issues. (Stake 1995, 133).

In our second year, when the question emerged as to whether the partnerships were supportive given the problems in our students' lives outside of school, we found the autobiographies to be important data in a different way than they were during the previous year. They provided needed information about what kind of mentors/teachers the eighth graders would be to their second-grade partners.

Informal Conversations About Students Become Data

> The question is what's the research for . . . Is it for us to feel successful, or is it to find out more about teaching and students? Sometimes what we find out doesn't make us feel very good. (Michelle, Research Meeting on May 15, 1995)

During the second year we discovered that the students were very different in their emotional needs from those who had participated in the first year. We realized that the information we were learning about students' lives outside of school was now a source of data that was impacting how we thought about the partnerships. While we did not originally think of conversations with students and their family members, school counselors, social workers, community contacts, and previous teachers as data, it became evident that information from these sources were what caused us to have new research questions. The data we were gathering about students' troubles outside of school led us to feel an urgent need to analyze the data we had collected on the partnerships. Whereas in our first year we waited until the summer to analyze data for evidence of academic benefits, in the second year we could not delay examining the data to see if the partnerships were emotionally supportive and if they should continue. This led us to quickly schedule a research day away from school to analyze the data we had collected thus far.

On a chilly winter day we sat in front of a blazing fire at Georgiana's house and read all the students' autobiographies and the letters they had exchanged. We read these autobiographies and letters aloud by assuming the roles of the partners. Using what we were learning about the lives of the students, we tried to imagine what they were experiencing through the partnership relationship.

After reviewing all the written exchanges between partners, we were able to document many positive elements of the partnerships. We could identify ways in which the students were meeting county and state curricular objectives. For example, they were exhibiting the ability to recognize and answer questions, and they had proofread and revised their writing so that their partner would understand what they wanted to communicate. There were many expressions of friendship, admiration, and appreciation in the writings exchanged between partners that we viewed as emotionally supportive. For example, to understand what the experience might be for each child, we read Samuel's autobiography and the letter Tyler wrote in response.

> Dear Samuel, Thank you for inviting me to your school. . . . You have good drawings. Thank you for helping [me]. I appreciated it. Your buddy, Tyler

The many expressions of caring between students renewed our faith in the partnership project. We saw the importance of continuing the partnerships and continuing to collect data that would be useful in monitoring whether students' academic and emotional needs were being met.

Class and Individual Interview Data

> Johni: I think with research we want them to do what we expect them to do [but] they are human beings that think on a different wave length and they don't come up with

what we expect. I get frustrated because they don't come up with what I thought they should or would have come up with.

Michelle: So what could we do differently so that we are able to follow their lead rather than having expectations that we hope they will realize?

Georgiana: We could ask them. (Research Meeting on May 15, 1995)

The exchange quoted above occurred toward the end of our second year of researching literacy partnerships. It has been interesting to observe how we have had to continue to remind ourselves of the importance of seeking students' perspectives in conducting our teacher research. Those who write about ethnography emphasize that "the field researcher watches for the sorts of things that are meaningful to those studied" (Emerson, Fretz, and Shaw 1995, 28). Teacher researchers are a very special kind of field researcher in that they are fully immersed in the world they are studying. In studying what occurs in their classrooms, they are continually challenged to find ways to better understand what is meaningful to their students. We sought student perspectives in the first and second year and now with some time and distance from the research we find ourselves able to describe the variety of ways in which this helped us keep students at the center.

Sometimes we conducted whole class discussions that served as *group interviews*. There were group interviews with the second-grade class and with the eighth-grade class. The purpose of the interviews in the first year of research was to get the students' opinions on what they thought should happen next between the partners, and what they would recommend we do with future partnerships. We took notes on what was said and/or audiotaped the interviews. At the end of the first year of the partnerships, we conducted a large-scale interview with both classes together. The views expressed by students were encouraging and provided us with new ideas to try the following year. For example, they suggested that next year's partners introduce themselves via video prior to writing autobiographies, that second graders write books for their eighth-grade partners, and that videotapes be made of eighth–grade literature discussions.

During the second year, the purpose of group and individual interviews altered as we focused on a new research question. When Johni had serious concerns about the eighth graders' commitment to their second grade partners, she conducted a group interview. She was prompted to conduct these interviews because of the confidential information she was hearing from Georgiana about the emotional instability in many of the second graders' lives. While this information could not be shared with the eighth grade partners, it became increasingly important to Johni to gather data on the eighth graders' commitment to upcoming partnership projects.

The most important group interview with the eighth graders occurred toward the end of the school year, at a time when Johni was questioning her students' commitment. Johni began the interview session by explaining that it was very important to understand the impact they as eighth graders had on the lives of the second graders. To assist them in thinking about this, Johni asked her students to tell a story about a personal experience in their schooling that was significant. They told stories about teachers who had done something special on their behalf and stories about teachers who had disappointed them. Johni used these stories to get the eighth graders to reflect on their roles as mentor/teachers to their second-grade partners. Finally, Johni asked them to go home and think about whether they wanted to prepare presentations of their final ecology projects for the second-grade class. The next day, the students were unanimous in deciding that they wanted to meet with the second graders again and to present their projects.

While the interview process is important to keeping students central to teacher research, we also have learned that it does not necessarily ensure that the students will all live up to what they have said, promised, or decided in a group interview. Nevertheless, seeking students' perspectives and getting their opinions through group interviews has been important to our research process.

We have also gathered helpful data through *individual interviews* at different times during the research. For example, Georgiana decided to conduct an interview with Tyler after he got a new partner mid-year when his former partner Samuel was returned to the Youth Detention Center because he stole a car. Georgiana told Tyler that Samuel would no longer be able to be his partner. When Tyler asked why, Georgiana felt it was important that Tyler understand that Samuel's absence had nothing to do with Tyler. She was honest with Tyler about Samuel's troubles outside of school. Johni arranged for Stuart, an eighth grader in one of her other classes, to join the research class so that he could be Tyler's literacy partner. Georgiana's purpose in conducting an individual interview was to understand Tyler's feelings in response to the change in partners. Did Tyler feel that both his partnerships were supportive?

Georgiana asked Tyler if he would talk with her for a short time about the literacy partnerships while other students were at their music class. Tyler agreed. They had had quiet talks before, so this was not an unusual situation. Sometimes Georgiana conducted interviews by inviting a child to sit with her briefly while the rest of the students continued their work. On this occasion she felt Tyler might be more comfortable without other students present.

Georgiana: Tyler, what did you think of your first partner, Samuel?

Tyler: Samuel, he was real nice. I liked meeting him. He helped me with my food in line at the party.

Georgiana: How did you feel when Samuel got into trouble and had to go to the Youth Detention Center?

Tyler: I didn't really believe it at first. I didn't think he would do that. I wasn't mad at him, but I was disappointed.

Georgiana: Did you want a new partner?

Tyler: At first I thought I wasn't going to get another partner. I felt lonely, kind of. He (Stuart) wrote me a letter telling me I was his new partner. I wanted to meet him. I thought he was a nice person. He invited me over to his house, but I couldn't come. I want to keep all Stuart's letters.

Georgiana: Do you think we ought to have partners next year in second grade?

Tyler: Yes, I think they ought to do partners. Can I still have a partner?

Georgiana: You could suggest that to your third-grade teacher. Do we need to make any changes in what we did this year?

Tyler: I think things should stay the same.

This interview gave Georgiana insight into Tyler's feelings. His remarks were candid and reassured her that the partnership with Samuel had not been damaging and the partnership with Stuart had been supportive. Teacher researchers often have an advantage in conducting interviews with students because of the rapport that hopefully has already been established between teacher and student. Glesne and Peshkin (1992), who write about becoming qualitative researchers, view rapport as "a distance-reducing, anxiety-quieting, trust-building mechanism that primarily serves the interest of the researcher" (p. 94). When teachers build positive relationships with their students, we are building rapport that serves more than research interests. Teachers have a unique advantage when it comes to conducting interviews because of the many opportunities we have to establish rapport, as well as the flexibility we have to conduct interviews more spontaneously whenever it becomes evident that information is needed to inform the research.

Concluding Thoughts

It may seem obvious that taking up teacher research is about learning what we as teachers can do that will benefit our students' intellectual, social, and civic development. Educational research is ideally intended to create knowledge that benefits students. However, collecting data according to the conditions deemed most appropriate to a prescribed method becomes the primary concern of many outsider researchers (e.g., university professors and doctoral students). Often what these researchers want to do in classrooms conflicts with the unpredictable complexities of day-to-day circumstances in the lives of children and their teachers. We submit that conducting teacher research is different because what matters most is what is best for the students at any moment in time. Thus the goals of the research must be continuously evaluated and accordingly revised in light of the students' best interests. If at any time some aspect of the research conflicts with student needs, then it is necessary to abandon, alter, or postpone the research.

In Richard Louv's book on the future of childhood, there are many stories told by parents and teachers about how society is failing to meet the needs of children. One teacher's description of the students he teaches speaks directly to why we think it is of utmost importance to keep the students at the center of teacher research.

> I have twenty-five children in my class. Twenty out of that twenty-five are on the free lunch program. That means they're below the poverty level. Twenty-two out of the twenty-five are minority, four are special ed, five are nonpro-motive, ten are bilingual, thirteen are at risk of dropping out. . . . People want changes—I think they ought to be asking me where the changes need to be. But instead, you get people like William Bennett [then Secretary of Education] up there telling me what works. Let him step into a class of twenty-five children that all seem to be having troubles, who all have needs and demands that come before academics—we're talking the real basics. (Louv 1990, 339)

We understand what this teacher is saying about "the real basics" because the challenges he recounts are like those we find in our classrooms. In learning how to incorporate research into the day-to-day events of our teaching lives, we find ourselves better able to cope with what worries us most about meeting our students' academic and basic needs. We expect new research questions each year and will continue to develop ways of keeping our students at the center of our teaching and researching processes. We are drawn to the idea that the researcher-researched relationship should be marked by negotiation, reciprocity, and a willingness on the part of all participants to change and be changed (Glesne and Peshkin, 1992). Through researching what matters most to us and our students, we have been encouraged, we have found answers, and we have gained hope. People have dealt with the unknown through research of all kinds. Given these difficult times, it may be research that enables us to continue as teachers who desperately want to do the best for our students.

References

Commeyras, M., J. Mathis, and G. Sumner. 1995. *Elementary and Middle School Partnerships: The Centrality of Relationships in Literacy Learning.* Instructional Resource No. 10. Athens, GA: NRRC, Universities of Georgia and Maryland College Park.

Emerson, R.M., R.I. Fretz, and L.L. Shaw. 1995. *Writing Ethnographic Fieldnotes.* Chicago: University of Chicago Press.

Glesne, C. and A. Peshkin. 1992. *Becoming Qualitative Researchers.* New York: Longman.

Herbert, B. 1996. "Turning Children's Rights into Reality." *The New York Times*: 21. 27 May 1996.

Louv, R. 1990. *Childhood's Future.* Boston: Houghton Mifflin.

Mendez, P. and C. Byard. 1989. *The Black Snowman.* New York: Scholastic.

Stake, R. 1995. *The Art of Case Study Research.* Thousand Oaks, CA: Sage.

Van Allsberg, C. 1981. *Jumanji.* Boston: Houghton Mifflin.

FIVE

The Importance of Research Relationships, the Power of a Research Community

Patti McWhorter, Barbara Jarrard,
Mindi Rhoades, Beth Tatum, and Buddy Wiltcher

When you open the door to a strange room, you never know what might be on the other side. Such a door opened for a group of us in the spring of 1993 when seven members of our fourteen-member English department accepted an invitation to join the School Research Consortium (SRC) of the National Reading Research Center (NRRC). As individuals we were all looking for answers to our teaching questions. We talked to each other about what was happening in our classrooms and what we wanted to try with our students, but we never thought of this interaction as research. Our step through that door, however, gave us a focus, a vehicle for testing our ideas, and a forum for sharing our ideas with others.

In the first meeting of the SRC, we sat in tiny chairs in the Fourth Street Elementary media center and looked at each other while Betty and JoBeth explained what the SRC might be. They had a vision; we could see that on their faces. They flashed wonderful professional books and articles, talked about research questions and data collection. They reassured us that we would not have to spend more time doing this research; we were already doing things that could fit naturally with what they were expecting. We agreed—to a point. With the longstanding commitment to professional growth in our department, we were accustomed to giving up personal time to enrich our lives as educators. We had designed and implemented several departmental staff development courses, developed an extensive professional library, and attended and presented at state conferences. But we had never designed our professional growth around formal research questions.

At our table, Mindi doodled. Buddy squirmed silently. Barbara and Sue smiled. Louise sat quietly, waiting. Beth whipped out her bag of Sweet Tarts and Blow Pops and distributed them. Patti selected a sour apple Blow Pop and tapped her pen on the blank legal pad. It was excruciating. We were in a new place in our relationship as department members, and we did not know what to expect.

"So, does anyone have any ideas?" Patti asked.

"Hey, you got us into this," Beth retorted, grinning slyly. Everyone giggled.

"Okay, what are you interested in? What's a problem in your classroom? What are you worried about with your kids?" Patti forged doggedly ahead.

"We need more multicultural literature," Louise offered.

"I am still working on my reading-with-an-adult-partner project," Beth added.

"I'm really following your lead on the peer evaluation and group projects, but I don't know the answers to a lot of my questions about this kind of teaching," Barbara said. Eyes turned to Mindi, Sue, and Buddy. We were clearly taking turns, offering everyone a chance to participate.

"Yeah," Mindi began. "I pretty much do what you suggest because I trust you as department chair, but I do have a lot of questions about keeping kids on task when we do group work. The noise level, the chaotic atmosphere sometimes—I mean, how can I control these things? *Can* I control these things?"

"It's like we know this kind of teaching—the group work and projects—is interesting and exciting to kids, but how do we organize all the directions they can go in and still know we are teaching what we are supposed to be teaching?" Sue pondered. Buddy nodded in agreement.

"All right, it looks like Barbara, Mindi, Sue, Buddy, and I may share some similar interests. Beth and Louise are interested in something different. Do we want to break up into some smaller groups?" Patti asked. More nods of agreement and the squeaking of chairs as we reconfigured our larger group.

We had made our first decision. Barbara, Buddy, Mindi, Sue, and Patti formed a small group within the larger departmental research group. Beth and Louise would pursue their own questions. Beth, however, planned to meet with our larger group on occasion because she was also interested in our questions, as well as her specific ones about the interaction between adult and adolescent reading partners. (Note: Sue had to leave our group when a new job took her to the school district's central office, and Louise eventually decided that the timing of the involvement with the SRC was not right for her personally.)

Our subgroup started by looking over the sample format for the research proposal we were expected to draft. As we puzzled over the task, we decided that in order to allow the members of the group to explore what was happening in each individual classroom, we needed to create broad research questions. Although we were at different points in terms of our years of teaching experience, this first formal discussion of our classrooms, our students, and our frustrations led us to the understanding that we shared similar approaches to instruction, and similar commitments to involving students in classroom decision-making. Specifically, we found that we had all been using project-based instruction to involve students more fully in classroom learning.

Sharing and discussing our experiences with projects helped us to realize that we had no hard evidence to support what we believed was a valuable and effective instructional approach. We discussed the possibility of giving the students more choices, developing these projects *with* students, rather than *for* students. This seemed a logical next step for us. If we were going to try something different anyway, why not find out if our instincts and inclinations were as effective as we believed them to be?

New Roles in the Professional Community

In our new roles as classroom researchers, we decided to focus our first efforts on broad questions framed within the context of student-generated curriculum:

- How will students who are given an opportunity to participate in generating their own curriculum respond?
- How will involvement in this activity affect their motivation to learn?

Developmentally as educators, we were all in different places relative to our age and experience. Mindi, the newest teacher among us, although inquisitive and less controlling by nature, struggled with the concern that she might not be teaching the correct content. Buddy, after eight years of teaching, was seeking new ways to approach instruction. His need for organization and structure in the classroom was diametrically opposed to Mindi's, yet they shared common beliefs about classrooms as communities of active learners. Barbara, whose fifteen years of teaching experience included a position in a more traditional and structured environment prior to her tenure at Cedar Shoals, was seeking new ways to challenge and involve her gifted students. For Patti, the journey to rethink and restructure her classroom began almost twelve years ago. All of us share the characteristic that bonds us closely as classroom researchers: We can never feel satisfied with the status quo. We can always see possibilities.

Collectively, we knew we were all bothered by the same questions about ourselves as teachers. How have we become who we are in our classrooms today? Why are we so driven to change, modify, and adapt our teaching? Why reinvent ourselves each year as teachers?

These questions, although not the subject of our individual research, strongly undergird our decision-making processes in the classroom. During the early stages of our work with the SRC, these shared concerns drew us together as a research community, although we were free to pursue our research individually.

The desire to work as a research team, however, helped us to discover our common ground—our interest in our students. In our earliest conversation as a formal team, we articulated our beliefs about students, classrooms, and our role as teachers in those classrooms. Through discussion and writing, we explored shared as well as divergent perspectives about our students, our level of trust in them, our interest in their needs, and our desire for their learning success. While we had often talked about these beliefs informally, writing them down helped us see how strongly we agreed on a basic philosophy of teaching, and gave us a touchstone for decisions throughout the year. We also knew that, in order to substantiate our beliefs, we needed to read what other educators were saying. As we discovered the similarities in our beliefs and those of the published "experts," we referenced these for each belief. As teachers new to classroom research, we wanted to be credible to others outside our immediate context. We eventually agreed on the following Belief Statement, based on our experience and bolstered by our reading:

1. We believe that students are intelligent enough to participate in steering their own educational experiences and that giving students the opportunity to do this increases their involvement in their education and their motivation to achieve and meet personal goals. (Zemelman, Daniels, and Hyde 1993)
2. We believe if students are motivated and involved in achieving educational goals, the level of classroom learning will meet or exceed standard, mandated curriculum requirements. Along with the teacher, students must become responsible for their own education and accountable for the end results. (Snyder, Lieberman, McDonald, and Goodwin 1992; Wigginton 1985)
3. We believe the primary role we play as teachers is to help students learn how to learn and how to take responsibility for their own learning. Through a student-centered curriculum, students develop a stronger sense of ownership and purpose. (Fawcett 1992; Moffett and Wagner 1992)
4. We believe teachers benefit by closer interaction with and a clearer understanding of students. Confrontations are replaced with consensus-building. (Atwell 1991; Chappel 1992)
5. We believe the community benefits by gaining independent learners who are able to function in a cooperative environment, solve problems, and think critically. (Kohn 1993)

In the early stages of our research, we knew that we had to define student-generated curriculum more clearly in order to research the issue. We found, however, that we could more precisely define what student-generated curriculum is *not*. It is *not* a teacher-guided, directed, and evaluated unit, project, or learning experience created in isolation of a knowledge of specific students in a specific classroom setting. It is *not* packaged sets of worksheets, lessons plans, and multiple choice tests used without considering the needs of a particular group of students in a specific classroom setting. Only in determining what was in opposition to student-generated curriculum could we more clearly articulate what characteristics it possesses.

As a research group, our early discussions revealed that we visualized classrooms and classroom activities on a continuum that spans from active to passive, paralleling student-centered to teacher-centered classrooms, and student-generated to teacher-generated curriculum.

As individual teachers, we were in different places on the continuum in terms of how we each developed and orchestrated classroom events (Foster 1993; Gere, Fairbanks, Howes, Roop, and Schaafsma 1992). Collectively, we recognized that the more productive place to be on the continuum, in terms of student learning, was in the direction of active learning, student-centered classrooms. In retrospect, this diversity strengthened our inquiry. It caused us to ask and answer difficult questions about the relationships that exist in classrooms between and among students and teachers. In our diverse classroom experiences, we continually struggle with issues that influence our teaching.

Given our shared beliefs and general direction of our goals, the projects were specific to our individual teaching situations and covered a range of topics:

- Patti's ninth-graders were interested in introducing eighth-graders to the challenges of high school through realistic scenarios they could read and discuss.
- Barbara's gifted students determined that they could reveal their knowledge of archetypes through an in-depth study of the movie *Star Wars* and the creation of a mural on the walls of the English wing.
- Mindi's lower-achieving seniors wanted their own senior newspaper and were willing to write grant applications to fund the newspaper's costs.
- Buddy's gifted tenth-grade students participated in the design and joint evaluation of a Utopia/Distopia project.
- Beth's students helped her see how to re-envision her project, which involved students reading and discussing novels with a parent or other adult partner outside of school, to approach the "lunch table book talk" that she found so valuable.

Our students and our individual comfort levels with these projects were clearly taking us in different directions, but the diversity in our project ideas (and students) helped us to realize more definitively that we cannot create "one size fits all" classrooms or classroom research projects. More importantly, as our students took us in these varied directions, we clung more closely together as researchers and found that the uncertainties of our first efforts did not seem so intimidating when we were able to discuss our concerns and questions with each other.

Looking back on our early experiences as classroom researchers, the power of our community is evident. Even though Beth continued to research her own questions, she met with our larger departmental group to discuss the process we were using, to give and receive support for her own work. Our insecurities about classroom research emerged early. What is data? Where is it? How do we deal with it? What must we do alike? What can be different? How do we triangulate data? (What *is* triangulating data?) Will anyone really want to know this? What if the end result of all of this work is nothing—no knowledge, no contribution to the profession?

Exploring our role in helping students participate in curriculum planning, and in Beth's case involving others outside the school, meant that we were compelled to gather data on our own actions and behaviors. Our plan books, teaching notes, and individual journals became important sources of data for tracking our own behaviors and reactions as well as those of our students. Monitoring student academic, social, and personal growth during the research process meant learning how to select student work samples, make anecdotal notes on student behaviors and reactions, tape and transcribe audio tapes, and track student achievement through our own assessment and evaluation systems.

In spite of our collective insecurities about research, we always believed in the power of our community as a department, and we intuitively trusted that working together on classroom research, something we were not entirely secure about, would work if we just stuck together. Joining the SRC convinced us that in telling our stories, other teachers might recognize their own varied classroom dilemmas and be able to improve learning experiences for their students. By Betty's and JoBeth's definition of classroom research, our struggles, questions, and findings could be meaningful to a wider audience.

Community as a Mindset

An outside observer of an SRC meeting would immediately label the Cedar Shoals research group as "disruptive." Like some of our students, we probably bring too much excess energy to the larger group meetings. We laugh, fidget, crack jokes, "high five" each other, and generally enjoy each other's company, sometimes to the horror of those who don't share our bizarre senses of humor. We jokingly refer to ourselves as a dysfunctional family, but family is the operative word here. This is not to say that we always understand and agree with each other; rather, we share a mutual respect for our individual strengths, and we are willing to help each other identify and work on the weaknesses in our teaching and research.

Individually, we might have abandoned everything. It was hard to face the larger SRC group and wonder if what we had done was worthwhile, if we had really made progress since the last meeting. Together, we found new energy and reasons to persevere. We discovered that our relationship as fellow researchers added depth and new meaning to our daily conversations. As we moved further along with our research, we grew accustomed to saying "Write that down—that might be important" in even the most casual conversations about our work.

As a research team, we found that we could channel and use our frustrations with teaching. What were formally obstacles and barriers in our teaching became points of discussion, possibilities for new directions with our research. New frustrations became new questions. New questions meant the possibility of fresh answers and new perspectives. In isolation from each other, we might have gravitated toward more negative and unproductive behaviors as teachers. Together, we were each other's cheerleaders and support, new sources of information and confirmation.

Perhaps the key factor in our ability to persevere as a collaborative research group was the kids we worked with everyday. Individually, we genuinely like working with adolescents. They exhaust and energize us. They make us laugh, and they make us cry. They are aggravating and intellectual and insightful. We kept plugging away because every instinct we had as teachers told us that through our research *together* we might find some answers to our most nagging questions about teaching.

Our nagging questions actually began as the stories we recounted about our kids and our classrooms when we met together as a team. We learned to claim these stories as part of our data, but only after we experienced a period of guilt for "wasting valuable research time." Through the stories we discovered some of our important questions: Are students wasting time when they talk to each other about classroom decisions or the development of projects? What about time off-task? How can teachers justify this messy process of inquiry? What are the most productive ways to organize classroom decision-making sessions? We began to find parallels between our adult behavior as a research group and the student behavior in groups in our classrooms. We brainstormed different strategies for dealing with this discovery by examining our own group.

"Look at us," Barbara remarked in one of our earliest group meetings. "We take a while to get cranked up each time we meet, and we certainly couldn't call ourselves 'on-task' all the time. Isn't it the same for our kids?"

"Yes, but we have to show that we have done something, accomplished something after we have met, don't we?" Buddy reminded us. "I mean, we have to go the SRC group this afternoon and talk about what we have done."

Discussion like this led us to a closer examination of the group dynamics at work in our classrooms. Patti, we knew, was the leader and timekeeper in the group. She organized the meetings, formalized the agendas, set deadlines (with input from the group), and acted as a liaison to the SRC. Other group members were responsible for action in their own classrooms and communicating their actions and the ensuing results to the larger group. We knew enough about structuring groups; what we were interested in was the accountability issue. We began to share ways to track the work of small groups and provide accountability for the students to us.

"Do you remember when we completed the staff development plan last year for instructional improvement, and I shared those daily logs and group work reports with you?" Patti asked. Everyone nodded. She continued, "I like using these kinds of forms to help students see what they are accomplishing in a group setting, but I would like a chance to reformulate and revise some of the forms to make them easier to use. I can already see how to add elements that they need to consider. For example, I now have them evaluate their group's efforts for a week and write down ways they can improve as a group. I added this to the form after I began to teach students how to be productive group members. And that's a goal we have, right? To help kids become more productive in group?"

We each had indeed been working toward that goal, in varying ways. Using the forms Patti shared as a foundation, members of our research group began to infuse varying forms of record-keeping for group work into daily lesson plans. Each subsequent research meeting became a place where we could report how these worked, what we would change, and what would remain the same. Our concern with accountability—knowing what our students were actually accomplishing in the learning experiences we orchestrated—became visible in the record-keeping forms we developed.

No longer were we tinkering with our own practice. Our influence reached the other teachers in our group, and consequently the lives of many students. Because we taught students who differed in age and ability, our discovery of common problems gave our research more meaning. Had we discovered issues in isolation of each other, we might have never recognized them.

Supportive Structures

At Cedar Shoals, our research group is blessed with a *common planning room* with other English teachers. In a larger building cursed by a crumbling infrastructure, we have a physical space that houses our desks, bookshelves, filing cabinets, computer, antiquated printer, phone, and up-to-date professional library. Not only does it house the physical aspects of our jobs, it also is a haven for our ideas and conversations. Almost any time of the day, someone in this planning room is willing to talk. From conversations about kids, the latest school gossip, book and movie reviews, to impromptu craft lessons, our planning room is a reflection of our lives.

Most importantly, it is a physical space that underscores our commitment to each other as teacher researchers.

Students are always a part of the conversation. Unlike the stereotypical view of conversations teachers are purported to have about kids, our sharing information about students has a supportive quality. Beth, our Student Support Team (SST) coordinator, is a helpful source of information. She knows as we do that the lives of students are often complicated, filled with treacherous events and complex relationships. As we work in our individual classrooms, we are often left with questions about what to do for students who seem so out of our reach of influence. Our interaction as department members reassures us that we are not alone in our struggles to make learning happen in our classrooms.

Since every student takes English for four years, our collegial atmosphere as a department and a research team means that a student is less likely to get lost among the 1500 we teach. We know who will struggle with state graduation tests, who will need to be recognized for extra effort in writing, and who needs to be nominated for awards. We share their stories as we eat lunch, make copies, prepare plans, and give makeup work. We mourn those who destroy their own potential through suicide or reckless living. And we celebrate when a student, after the fourth attempt, passes the state writing test. We cannot imagine doing the difficult job we do as classroom teachers without the support of our colleagues.

As much as the planning room is a blessing, it has also become an item of contention among the teachers who have attended our conference presentations and discussions of our research. We always have to apologize for having a planning room, which has forced us to ask ourselves, "Would we work this way as a research group without that common space?" The answer is emphatically "yes." The planning room is only a physical representation of who we are as educators and teacher researchers. The planning room did not force us to want to grow professionally, to want to become teacher researchers, and to want to work together. It is a symbol of our community, but it is not the reason we chose to work together.

Meetings and conversations are an integral part of our day. In addition to planning–room conversations, we conduct what we consider to be real research discussions and collaborations in our classrooms after school and in the hallway. Some of our classrooms are located on the same hall, and the proximity helps when we want to share our successes, failures, problems, and frustrations. "Come see this," Buddy beckons those of us in the hallway after class to his room. A student's spectacular artwork, in response to a piece of literature his class is studying, is spread over the desks. We celebrate the individual successes together. Mindi, Barbara, and Beth rendezvous in the hallway to discuss how having a cut-and-paste editing session might help Mindi's students see writing organization for the articles in their senior newspaper in a new way. Our deeply entrenched tradition of sharing and collaboration was in place long before we were linked by our collaborative research, but we can see in hindsight how our research was undergirded by that tradition.

We firmly believe that other groups of teachers can find what we have found through our collaboration if they are willing to find colleagues who share their philosophies, their views of students, and their curiosities and concerns. Like a good friendship, these relationships take time and effort. If they are important to us, however, we are usually willing to work on them.

It's important to note that in early discussions about joining the SRC, several department members were interested but made decisions not to join or not to continue after the initial meetings. Those who remained a part of the group did not interpret this as unprofessional. The process of becoming a teacher researcher varies for individuals, even for those who chose to remain part of the group. The spirit of inquiry, the joy of discovering new things about students and learning, a level of comfort with not knowing answers—these are crucial to becoming a classroom researcher. But many good teachers who do not identify themselves as researchers also possess these qualities.

The SRC as a funded project provided us with several *release days* for working on our research. Release days for classroom teachers who must prepare substitute plans, worry about how students will do in their absence, and return sometimes to the Armageddon of the day after a substitute are both a blessing and a curse. We chose to see them as a blessing, although some days this was hard. As a community of researchers, we learned to pull away from our day-to-day routines to examine and discuss our process as researchers and to share our stories. Given the constraints of a school day, and the distractions that take place in a building, we had to leave the building.

Becoming teacher researchers under the official auspices of the National Reading Research Center has validated what we know we have always done as a department: to think reflectively about what we do and work to improve our relationships with our students, our instructional practices, and our communication with the larger school community. The results of our research and our interactions with other researchers outside our school has given us a power we had never experienced. We feel driven to share the work we have completed and compelled to continue research in the future.

Perhaps the labor and birth analogy might help others see how we view our collaborative research experience. We conceived an idea, nurtured it as it developed, and gave birth to it in the form of publications (McWhorter, Jarrard, Rhoades, and Wiltcher 1996, 1997) and presentations at state and national meetings with support from the SRC. Our experiences with *publishing our work*, although the actual writing proved difficult at times, increased our commitment to informing the profession. We want other students to have the very positive experiences our own have had as we approached teaching in new ways. We are researchers now in every sense of the word.

New Confidence, New Questions

As researchers, we have gained enough confidence to venture out on our own with individual questions. Buddy and Beth are beginning to examine the effects of a culminating senior research project on our graduating seniors. They wonder if students will be able to produce the quality of work the department expects of its graduates. Barbara continues to expand and fine-tune the methodology she used with the *Star Wars* project; her interest lies in ways to utilize this approach with other students she teaches. Mindi is looking at options for expanding and improving the research process and the research products required of her eleventh-grade students. Patti is interested in involving students more closely in the classroom research process, inviting them to examine their own efforts more closely.

Although the first part of our journey together as a research group is over, we know the power of classroom research. Each of us is secure in the knowledge that we can come home to the "research family" we have created to seek guidance, share our successes, and find comfort when we meet with obstacles too difficult to handle individually in our teaching. This security has nurtured in each of us a sense of our own self-worth as educators; we feel a new sense of confidence about inquiry. Inquiry no longer belongs to the university researcher. Inquiry belongs to us, our students, and to anyone who wants to join us in discovering more about how our students learn.

References

Atwell, N. 1991. *Side by Side*. Portsmouth, NH: Heinemann.

Chappel, D. 1992, Fall. "The Stories We Tell: Acknowledging Emotion in the Classroom." *ADE Bulletin*: 20–23.

Fawcett, G. 1992, March. "Moving the Big Desk." *Language Arts*: 183–185.

Kohn, A. 1993, September. "Choices for Children: Why and How to Let Students Decide." *Phi Delta Kappan*: 8–19.

McWhorter, P. with B. Jarrard, M. Rhoades, and B. Wiltcher. 1996. *Student-generated Curriculum: Lessons from our Students*. Athens, GA: National Reading Research Center, The University of Georgia.

McWhorter, P. with B. Jarrard, M. Rhoades, and B. Wiltcher. 1997, Fall. "Student-generated Curriculum: Lessons from Our Students." *Connections: Georgia Language Arts*. Athens, GA: Georgia Council of Teachers of English.

Moffett, J. and B.J. Wagner. 1992. *Student-centered Language Arts, K–12*. Portsmouth, NH: Boynton/Cook/Heinemann.

Snyder, J., A. Lieberman, M.B. McDonald, and A.L. Goodwin. 1992. *Makers of Meaning in a Learning-centered school: A Case Study of Central Park East Elementary School*. New York: NCREST.

Wigginton, E. 1985. *Sometimes a Shining Moment*. New York: Anchor Press/Doubleday.

Zemelman, S., H. Daniels, and A. Hyde. 1993. *Best Practice: New Standards for Teaching and Learning in America's Schools*. Portsmouth, NH: Heinemann.

SIX

Extended Engagements: Learning from Students, Colleagues, and Parents

JoBeth Allen and Betty Shockley Bisplinghoff

A primary strength of teacher research is the first-hand perspective of the researcher. Teachers are immersed in the rich contexts of the classroom, integral to the lives of the participants, invested in the research questions, and intent on developing insights and strategies that will improve the teaching/learning relationship. As valuable as we believe the teacher researcher's perspective to be, we were struck by Goodson's (1995) challenge that teachers' stories need not only to be told, but to be socially and morally contextualized. Teacher narratives, a predominant form of teacher research, may accept or even celebrate existing power relations, Goodson argued, unless teachers broaden their perspectives by seeking multiple perspectives on that experience.

While many of us initially struggle to listen to and value our own voices (Gitlin, Bringhurst, Burns, Cooley, Myers, Price, Russell, and Tiess 1992), we extend our engagement by listening to the voices of others who can inform our practice: Colleagues, parents, and especially students. Valuing the experiences and perspectives of others in constructing one's own knowledge has been termed "connected knowing" by Belenky, Clinchy, Goldberger, and Tarule (1986):

> Connected knowers develop procedures for gaining access to other people's knowledge. At the heart of these procedures is the capacity for empathy. Since knowledge comes from experience, the only way they can hope to understand another person's ideas is to try to share the experience that has led the person to form the idea. . . . (p. 113)

This chapter explores the SRC community of researchers, and their attempts to add to their own perspectives on teaching and learning—to become connected knowers. We draw on periodic progress reports written by SRC researchers as well as observational notes from research team meetings, so the extended engagements are represented by the teacher researchers themselves through their talk and writing. We have continually fed back our interpretations to participants for their verification, special sensitivities, refutations, and new interpretations (Glesne and Peshkin 1992).

Research Community Perspectives

Studying within a group of teacher researchers provides a constant forum for considering the perspectives of others. Writing about his experience as a member of a "community of inquiry," Gordon Wells noted that "collaboration with colleagues is an important dimension of teacher research" because it provides "opportunities to meet with colleagues to make sense of the research experience by talking it over with others who understand it at first hand" (Wells, Bernard, Gianotti, Keating, Konjevic, Kowal, Maher, Mayer, Moscoe, Orzechowska, Smieja, and Swartz 1994, 33). We have written elsewhere (Allen and Shockley 1996) of the value of "interpretive dialogue"—talking about data. Researchers in the SRC found that the time to talk with each other about what they were experiencing was one of the most meaningful ways to broaden their individual perspectives.

Over the three years, many of the projects in the SRC were collaborative research teams from two to five teachers, with some including a media specialist, principal, or university-based researcher. SRC members who originally collaborated as much for support as by design reported the importance of the added perspective of working closely with peers. In writing about the formation of her five-member research team, English teacher Patti McWhorter (1995) explained:

> The decision was not made out of our ability to see into the future and predict that our work together would be more powerful, our decisions more complex and important, and our results applicable to a wider range of students and classrooms. It was a decision made because we like each other, and we share similar beliefs about teaching and learning. (p. 1)

The SRC met as a whole team every six to eight weeks throughout the year and for whole days during the summers. During these meetings, teacher researchers made connections, formed collaborations, shared resources and analytic strategies, and exercised the rare opportunity to talk with teachers who have different teaching and research perspectives. These perspectives come from differing experiences, philosophies, years of teaching, and contexts. Over the three years of its existence, the SRC included teachers from small urban and rural areas; elementary, middle school, high school, and universities; and media centers, special education, art, and regular classrooms.

At a summer 1994 meeting for research analyzing and writing, a diverse group consisting of a high school English teacher, a university teacher, a middle school English teacher, and a second grade teacher had a lively discussion about recent trends in literacy education, characterized alternately as "progressive" and "experimental and trendy." The high school teacher believed that "middle school students are coddled and protected, not prepared for the hostile environment of high school." Someone countered that maybe the high school environment shouldn't be so hostile. One invoked the name of Atwell with reverence, another with scorn. In another conversation, two teachers whose project had led them to think about the effects of tracking in their high school chatted with an elementary teacher and a university teacher. Their talk was not academic, but parental. They shared their discomfort with the incongruence of their educational ideals and their perspectives as parents of high performing students. No one had any answers. But everyone agreed on one thing: As educators, we need to talk with each other across schools and levels to figure out better ways to support students during transitions from elementary to middle school, and from middle school to high school.

The opportunity to talk with other teachers about classroom data is one of the primary strengths of teacher research communities. Veteran teacher researcher Judy Buchanan shared the writing of fourth-grader Anwar with colleagues at several points during the year. In her case study, she wrote, "Through looking closely at his work and reflecting with others, I found some new ways to support his learning in the classroom" (Cochran-Smith and Lytle 1993, 220). Our membership in the SRC community, our reading of teacher research reports, interviews with them about becoming researchers, and observation of interactions lead us to agree with Judy Buchanan:

> The opportunity to ask questions and to reflect on one's work is essential to learning regardless of the age of the learner. Sharing my questions with my colleagues and in turn listening to more voices enlarged and deepened the conversation about teaching. (p. 220)

Student Perspectives

The people who know the most about learning (or not learning) in school are students. While student insights have been largely ignored in studies of classrooms, recent work holds promise of strategies that tap student perspectives. Oldfather enlisted students as co-researchers in longitudinal inquiry on their own motivation to learn (Oldfather and McLaughlin 1993); Alvermann et al. (1995) tapped students' perceptions of how they experienced text discussion; and Hudson-Ross, Cleary, and Casey (1993) created narratives in children's own voices, without adult analysis, to hear their perceptions about literacy learning.

How do we get inside student thinking? How do we look through their eyes? Almy and Genishi (1959, 1979), early advocates of teachers as action researchers, recommend asking children about themselves, observing them in a variety of settings, and studying children through others (especially parents). The process of involving students as active participants in the inquiry process not only provides teachers with valuable insights, it also can lead to deepened self awareness on the part of the students.

SRC members can point to many ways in which their students are benefitting from the literacy practices under study. However, the focus of this report is on what teachers learned about students through researching their own practices. Teachers learned from their students and made changes.

High school English teacher Louise Neal solicited her students' help in reviewing books by African-American authors to increase the diversity of the predominantly white-American literature reading list. In an interview with Betty, Louise explained that she was using NRRC funds to buy classroom books by African-American authors, but not just any book. She wanted literature with "inspiring life models" like James Comer's *Maggie's American Dream* because "it shows a Black family with those dreams, those aspirations . . . That's what I want to impart to the students." The method she created involved students by having them critique a broad range of books and make decisions about what would be on the reading list for future classes. Through their critiques and choices, students began to broaden Louise's perspective. She did not want to include books about slavery, share-croppers, or other examples of victimization. However, "students told me that [these books are] something that . . . they should read, that they should know about." Students who read all of Maya Angelou's books loved *I Know Why the Caged Bird Sings*, but told Louise, "Hey, look, don't ask students to read all those books on that woman's life. . . . She should not have taken that long to tell her story." Louise learned that her criteria for good literature and her students' were different, and she modified the reading list taking both perspectives into consideration.

Beth Tatum (Chapter 5, this volume) loves to read and talk about books with her colleagues. The English teachers at her high school have a work room where they have lunch and talk about books, regularly and informally. She wrote:

> [We] talk about the characters as if they are real people. . . . When I read *Dixie Riggs* by Sara Gilbert, . . . I knew [my co-workers] would find the main character humorous. So I read to them from the chapter that begins, "I think I'm a redneck. I'm not sure I'm a redneck, but I think I am as I stand here in my leather skirt and fake fur coat." . . . I gave them daily updates on her life and adventures. . . . But the conversation at lunch is really lively when two or more teachers are familiar with the same book. (Tatum, 1995, 1)

Beth used her perspective as a member of a reading community to reflect on her classroom reading communities. She wanted her students to experience the same kind of lively, authentic talk about books. "But in my classroom . . . all talk about literature looked like school talk" (p. 3). She decided the setting was the problem, "so I moved the discussion of novels out of the classroom and into the home. If students discussed novels with someone other than the teacher, I hoped they would not feel compelled to use school talk" (p. 4). She asked students to read a novel with a parent or other adult family member, discuss it, record the discussions, and reflect on similarities and differences in reader responses.

As a researcher, Beth has been most interested in her students' perspectives on this reading experience, and their reflections on "how powerful a small discussion about a novel can be in the life of a family" (p. 8). One student, in reading and discussing *Sleeping with the Enemy* with her mother, learned her grandfather had been an abusive husband and father. Another young woman came to a startling insight about her father. She reported that "I always thought my father was stupid because he never went to college," but discovered in reading *Dances with Wolves* together that her father "read like an English teacher," explaining things to her and making connections that she had missed.

A mother and son reading *The Autobiography of Malcolm X* had very different reactions. The son told Beth that his mother had been very calm and reflective about what Malcolm X stood for and the changes he went through. However, the student felt a sense of passion mixed with rage. He wanted to do something about the injustices in this world, particularly the injustices facing black males. His mother shared her initial response to the book when she read it for the first time as a teenager, a reaction very much like her son's. The book opened an important dialogue about their individual actions and reactions to racial injustice (Tatum 1995, 24).

Beth not only gained a new perspective on book talk, but her students had new ways of viewing their parents as readers. "I had provided them with the opportunity for a meaningful learning experience that moved beyond just the discussion and into their private lives," Beth reported (Tatum 1995, 11).

Learning how to gather and reflect on student perspectives is evolving. Chapter 1 math teacher Sherry MacDonald had students create their own word problems, in hopes that they would overcome their anxiety about this nemesis of many struggling students. She asked the students to report on the effectiveness of the process by using smiley faces to answer several questions, but in retrospect she was dissatisfied. "I would have learned much more by simply having them explain in their own words how they felt," she decided.

Parent Perspectives

In the SRC, we are learning from teacher researchers elsewhere the importance of listening to families. Robin Headman, fourth-grade teacher researcher in Norristown, Pennsylvania, asked parents to join her in an investigation of their children's reading and writing both in and out of school. Together they observed, documented, analyzed, and interpreted. They found that their diverse perspectives not only enriched the learning for them as researchers, but also created strong, supportive relationships. Headman urges other teacher researchers to include parents as active coinvestigators:

> Together, parents and teachers might find new ways to talk about children's literacy, new ways to interact with children, new relationships between home and the school, or new questions to ask about children' literacy in and out of school. (Cochran-Smith and Lytle 1993, 230)

Several SRC projects have extended beyond the classroom and into homes, including a family history art project (Easom, Eisenman, and Harvell 1994) and Tatum's shared book reading project. Karen Hankins' study (1994; Chapter 2, this volume) was designed to incorporate the perspectives of the parents of three kindergarten children she taught, children exposed prenatally to alcohol and/or cocaine. After studying the research literature on children affected by drugs in utero, Karen searched for a more connected kind of knowing. She wrote,

> I found some evidence of my children in those articles but nowhere did I find a complete description of any of them, and certainly not of the three of them together. I felt validated in my role as a researcher because I could tell the world about three children who were not well-described in the medical or special education journals. (p. 3)

Karen began making home visits, talking with relatives when children were staying with them rather than parents, and offering literature dialogue journals, which families used sporadically. She learned about drug relapses, incarceration, hospitalization because "the alcohol has eat up my liver," and a mother who had gone on "vacation." But she learned of these troubles from other family members who had stepped in to care for the children. Karen reflected:

> One of the studies [said] that parents who are addicted are "primarily committed to the drug and the child's needs are neglected." The authors . . . summarized by stating that children of substance abusing parents are living in unstable, often dangerous environments, cared for inconsistently. . . . (Howard et al. 1989). I thought about that long and hard. Were my children being neglected? Were they inconsistently cared for? Not really. In every situation someone in the family wrapped their arms around these children and kept them afloat. . . . While it's tragic that their parents are impaired by substance abuse, my children were always loved by extended family. . . . In every interview with the birth parents I read love and hope in their eyes as they talked about their children. (Hankins 1994, 5)

Her insights led Karen to redefine family and to see the children "through the eyes of their first teachers," their parents, and extended families. She began to understand a culture very different from hers and to understand her own cultural heritage. Donna Alvermann (1993) argued that "we as researchers need to . . . explain how our own background experiences will likely influence what we find and report in our writing" (p. 4) rather than hide behind the "muted voices" of impersonal, academic writing. Karen had to place herself in her research, and the families of her three students helped her.

> Reflecting on the present took me on a journey through the past. In walking the struggles of these children and their families I revisited my call to teaching. I stripped it of its purity and found needs in myself that had held me back at times from seeing children honestly. As I connected to the families of my children, I realized that I could never fully embrace their culture until I was willing to embrace my own. For the first time *ever* I found myself listening to my family stories and claiming with pride those mill-hill legends and "lint head" dialects.

Conclusion

Through their membership in and study of communities of teacher researchers, Marilyn Cochran-Smith and Susan Lytle (1993) concluded, "In communities that support teacher research . . . teachers may be willing to confront their own histories, hear the dissonance within their own profession, and begin to construct working alliances with colleagues, students, parents, and communities" (p. 84). Teachers in the SRC are developing these alliances, both within and beyond the classroom walls. There has been an expansion of perspectives within the SRC, widening the circles of perception out from the individual, creating and supporting connected knowing.

References

Alvermann, D. 1993. "Researching the Literal: Of Muted Voices, Second Texts, and Cultural Representations. In *Examining Central Issues in Literacy Research, Theory, and Practice*, ed. D. Leu and C. Kinzer. Forty-second Yearbook of the National Reading Conference. Chicago: NRC.

Alvermann, D., J. Young, D. Weaver, K. Hinchman, D. Moore, S. Phelps, E. Thrash, and P. Zalewski. 1995. *Middle- and High-school Students' Perceptions of How they Experience Text-based Discussions: A Multicase Study.* Athens, GA: National Reading Research Center, Reading Research Report No. 36.

Baumann, N., C. Fuentes, and J. Holman. 1994. *Reading Buddies.* Unpublished report. Athens, GA.

Cochran-Smith, M., and S.L. Lytle, eds. 1993. *Inside/Outside: Teacher Research and Knowledge.* New York: Teachers College Press.

Commeyras, M., J. Mathis, and G. Sumner. 1995. *Elementary and Middle School Partnerships: The Centrality of Relationships in Literacy Learning.* Athens, GA: National Reading Research Center, Instructional Resource No. 10.

Easom, M., G. Eisenman, and D. Harvell. 1994. *The Family History Art Book Project: Implementation and Evaluation.* Unpublished report. Athens, GA.

Gitlin, A., K. Bringhurst, M. Burns, V. Cooley, B. Myers, K. Price, R. Russell, and P. Tiess. 1992. *Teachers' Voices for School Change: An Introduction to Educative Research.* New York: Teachers College Press.

Glesne, C., and A. Peshkin. 1992. *Becoming Qualitative Researchers.* White Plains, NY: Longman.

Goodson, I. 1995, January. *Representing Teachers: Identity and Context.* Paper presented at the Conference on Qualitative Research in Education. Athens, GA.

Hankins, K. 1994, December. *Creating Literate Relationships with Fetal-alcohol and/or Crack Affected Children and Their Families.* Paper presented at the National Reading Conference. San Diego, CA.

Hudson-Ross, S., L. Cleary, and M. Casey. 1993. *Children's Voices: Children Talk About Literacy.* Portsmouth: Heinemann.

Jarrard, B. 1995. Untitled draft of report on student-generated curriculum project. Unpublished manuscript. Athens, GA.

Keffer, A., S. Carr, B. Lanier, L. Mattison, D. Wood, and R. Stanulis. 1994. "Teacher Researchers discover magic in forming an adult writing workshop." *Language Arts* 73(2): 113-121.

McWhorter, P. 1995. Untitled draft of report on student generated curriculum project. Unpublished manuscript. Athens, GA.

McWhorter, P., B. Jarrard, M. Rhoades, and B. Wiltcher, B. 1996. *Student-generated Curriculum: Lessons from our Students.* Athens, GA: National Reading Research Center, Instructional Resource No. 30.

Oldfather, P. and J. McLaughlin. 1993. "Gaining and Losing Voice: A Longitudinal Study of Students' Continuing Impulse to Learn Across Elementary and Middle Level Contexts." *Research in Middle Level Education* 17: 1–25.

Tatum, B. 1995. *Capturing Authentic Conversations About Literature.* Unpublished research report. Athens, GA.

Wells, G., L. Bernard, M. Gianotti, C. Keating, C. Konjevic, M. Kowal, A. Maher, C. Mayer, T. Moscoe, E. Orzechowska, A. Smieja, and L. Swartz. 1994. *Changing Schools from Within: Creating Communities of Inquiry.* Portsmouth, NH: Heinemann.

SEVEN

Potential Engagements: Dialogue Among School and University Research Communities[1]

JoBeth Allen and Betty Shockley Bisplinghoff

The School Research Consortium was an extension of our work together as a collaborative action research team (with Barbara Michalove) as we investigated and wrote *Engaging Children* (Allen, Michalove, and Shockley, 1993) and *Engaging Families* (Shockley, Michalove, and Allen, 1995). We experienced tremendous mutual benefits from our research relationships. JoBeth learned from master teachers and gained credibility with her university students by being in classrooms on a regular basis; she was rewarded by the university for the related grants, presentations, and publications; and she engaged in exciting, generative problem solving regarding teacher research methodology. Betty had opportunities to appreciate and use her vantage point as a teacher to design research, to observe first-hand the methods of an experienced university researcher, and to learn beyond her classroom, broadening her understanding through attending conferences and consulting with other teacher researchers. We particularly value the lasting friendships as well as collegial relationships and are continuing our work together.

With the formation of the SRC, we hoped to support other researchers in forming fruitful research relationships. We also hoped to bring our two primary communities, the schools and the university, closer together. This book represents the formation of many fruitful research relationships. Uniting school and university communities might take a little longer but holds tremendous potential.

This chapter examines that potential, some obstacles, and what researchers in schools, universities, and funding agencies might do to move towards key principles of mutual understanding and respect. These keys are critical in unlocking windows and doors in these literal and metaphorical buildings. Once

---

1. This chapter is shortened and modified from a previously-published article (Allen and Shockley 1996), which was in turn based on an invited, collaborative keynote address at the Conference on Qualitative Research in Education, Athens Georgia, January 6, 1995.

the doors are open, we may even be able to build a wide corridor connecting three groups of people who share an important goal: The improvement of literacy education.

Time and Priorities

At universities, if research and scholarship are not a priority, we don't get to stay. The situation is reversed in schools. There, if teaching is not a priority, we do not get to stay. The first, and in some schools the only, priority is teaching. Research must be on the teacher's own time, an added activity rarely valued or even acknowledged by evaluators. Both research communities are in need of continuity, integration, and synergy. How might we learn from each other?

Many university researchers have been enculturated to develop straight *lines of research*, with each study building on the last. Promotion and tenure committees expect interests to remain relatively stable; eyebrows twitch if the researcher appears "unfocused." University researchers often have the stress of several research projects moving along that line, but in different stages. We move (or at least pray that we move) from idea to proposal to funding to site selection to research to conference presentations to publication. But midway through this year's project, the prodigious university researcher is already developing next year's proposal.

In contrast, teacher researchers must be led by the *lives of research*: students. Writing a proposal in one year for the following year is rarely good teacher research, because in the teacher research tradition, questions and methods grow out of the specific context. Teachers don't look for research sites; they live in them. Because each group of students is unique, the research questions may change, opportunities for data collection may be different, and ongoing analysis or reflection may change teaching decisions, altering the whole study. While teacher researchers like Carol Avery, Nancie Atwell, and Vivian Paley have developed focused bodies of research and reflection, their first priority is always to the children and contexts in which they live. Paley eloquently explained, "Such is the way life in the classroom reinterprets the research. Whatever else I may choose to watch and record, my subjects draw me into deeper concerns and more vivid visions of their world" (1990, 19).

In addition to differing priorities (some chosen, some forced) there are issues of time. Teachers in the SRC were concerned about the potential for their roles as teachers and researchers to conflict. New teacher researchers especially struggle to make research an organic part of their teaching days, examining what they *already* do, collect, and interpret. Sometimes it is just overwhelming to even consider researching one's teaching.

Emily Carr, an experienced researcher in her kindergarten classroom, moved to third grade. She planned a study with Sally Hudson-Ross, who was teaching high school English for a year in a job exchange after having been a college professor for nearly a decade. They talked about their demanding new jobs and the planned project that was falling by the wayside. SRC members urged them to write about their struggles so others might benefit from their experiences. These veteran researchers balked:

> It is hard enough to do any research as a teacher. It is even harder when you are doing something new. It is . . . almost impossible when what you are doing is not going well. . . . "The Teacher Researcher has a Nervous Breakdown" may be interesting to read, but not to live through.

School-based researchers are not the only ones who feel these wrenching demands on time and priorities. Michelle Commeyras, an assistant professor at UGA, has been an active collaborator within the SRC. However, an individual research project in the NRRC rather than a collaborative one in the SRC would literally have bought her more time. On a solo project, she could have asked for release time from teaching and/or for summer salary in lieu of teaching summer school. Either would have given her more time to write. Strongly committed to collaborative action research, she also knew she must use her time wisely to succeed at the university. How do researchers in these two settings, with different but equally conflicting demands on time, make choices? It is encouraging to us, and to other university faculty who engage in collaborative research with teachers, that Michelle's work was valued at the university community; she did become an associate professor, and was awarded a Fullbright to work in South Africa.

Funding agencies have their own priorities and time issues. In recent years professional organizations including the International Reading Association and the National Council for Teachers of English, as well as at least one private foundation (the Spencer Foundation), have established teacher research grants. As mentioned previously, the federal government for the first time provided major funding for teacher research with the NRRC grant. Funding agencies have boards, missions, timetables, and often product specifications. These may or may not match school rhythms of beginning and ending, teaching and testing. In addition to time issues, funding agencies and schools may have conflicting priorities. Officials from one foundation recently confided to a group of teachers that while they believed wholeheartedly in the value of teacher research, and understand how much time it takes to develop a research team, questions, and methodologies, there are others in the foundation who do not and who may be applying standards that are more appropriate for other researchers.

What can we learn from each other? What we have in common is the need to balance teaching and research and still have some time for the rest of our lives. One step the Spencer Foundation has taken is to create different kinds of grants, one a "capacity building grant" designed to help teachers develop classroom research skills. NCTE and IRA include teachers on the committees that developed the original proposal guidelines. Some teacher research groups have benefitted from working closely with university researchers like Ruth Hubbard, Brenda Power, and Dixie Goswami, who have devoted much of their professional lives to working with such groups. These resource people are able to share experiences of other researchers from schools throughout the country.

Learning and Generating Methodology

Methodology and research design is an area that has strong potential for school-based and university-based researchers to learn from each other. This is also where the widest gulf is for many in both communities.

In their research proposals, SRC teachers wrote what they planned to do and why the questions were important. Some reviewers pushed them to write exactly how they were going to collect and analyze data, believing that the funding agency would reject the entire proposal without those details. That expectation is in direct contrast to the changing nature of research design and methodology in teacher research (Cochran-Smith and Lytle 1993; Hubbard and Power 1993). One reviewer ranked the proposals from 1 to 10, judging some "too vague, undefined, and amorphous to be supported," some "completely impossible in current form." The reviewer wrote comments such as "Why is this an important question?" on a study of teenagers and adults reading and talking together about books; "no evidence that this works as a data collection approach" about a plan to tape record book-buddy conversations; and "is it reliable? doubtful pre-post or post-post comparisons" for a proposed portfolio assessment. The reviewer flatly rejected Karen Hankins' proposal to combine case study and memoir to generate an intensely personal methodology, telling her that the only memoirs people are interested in reading are of presidents. Other university researchers were tremendously excited by the potential of Karen's new methodology. Karen's work resulted in a chapter in this volume, which will also be published by *Harvard Educational Review*.

On the other hand, the methodologies of university-based researchers often seem inaccessible or unrealistic to school-based researchers. Most teachers have not been trained as academic researchers, and seldom have the background in sociolinguistic analysis, ethnographic interviewing, or regression analysis. Teacher researchers rarely take detailed field notes for any length of time, or control variables for reliable experimental comparisons.

What could these two research communities learn about methods from each other? We draw on our own experiences and those of SRC members to explore that question.

Engaging Children. With our colleague Barbara Michalove, then a second-grade teacher, we studied six children from Barbara's and Betty's classrooms and their literacy development through three years of school (Allen, Michalove, and Shockley 1993). Many of our methods grew out of our weekly data-analysis discussions. In the beginning, Barbara and Betty worried that to be considered "real researchers" they should be taking the kind of detailed notes JoBeth wrote; she, after all, was "the expert." They even tried it—briefly. The result was intense frustration, sending them in search of meaningful but manageable methods. They came up with individual ways of detailing their decision-making as teachers, and documenting their students' literacy development. This took time, however, and constant experimentation, learning from each other, and learning from reading what other teacher researchers did. They began seeing and using classroom processes and records as data: student conference logs, reading inventories, and daily writing. Both found ways of jotting brief notes of key events that fit their teaching rhythms.

As a team, we had different and valuable perspectives as insiders and out-
siders:

Betty: *I was there when* Joseph decided he didn't need to go to his special education class every day, and when Shannon told me all the ways she had thought
of to kill herself.

JoBeth: *When I was there* I captured the children's conversations, details of reading
and writing in progress, and discussions with the children's other teachers outside the classroom.

Through JoBeth's written documentation, Betty and Barbara could *be there*
again and again. Moments heretofore lost or imperfectly recalled were now sys-
tematically captured for reexamination and poised for inclusion in a growing body
of daily experiences we began to call data. Together, we had a design stronger than
an observational study with "key informants."

Drawing on our different backgrounds and perspectives, we constructed responsive methods. For example, when a data-analysis session focusing on the
quarterly interviews JoBeth did with each child revealed that at least one child
was "putting her on," Barbara suggested that she take over the interviewing, incorporating the questions into her daily reading and writing conferences. Barbara
knew the children better and was able to embed questions in a logical instructional framework and interpret responses in the full context of the classroom. The
study had a built-in triangulation of perspectives.

Engaging Families. These multiple perspectives were even more important in
our second study (Shockley, Michalove, and Allen 1995). We examined connections between home and school that Betty fostered with a set of "parallel practices" she developed in first grade, and Barbara continued with the same children
and families in second grade. We studied home-school journals, written family stories, oral stories, and other artifacts. JoBeth had been studying grounded theory
and suggested that we try the fine-grained coding of the constant comparative
method. We spent several full days reading about the methodology, coding four
sets of transcripts together, and generating an extensive code list. We agreed to
code the other sets on our own and meet weekly to compare our analyses.

We were all unhappy with the process. Betty came to the next meeting with a
new plan. We agreed that we were losing the children, their families, and the real
stories by reducing these rich exchanges to codes. Betty suggested, and we immediately adopted, a plan to read all the data about one child/family unit independ-
ently, write a one- to three-page narrative interpretation, and come together
weekly to read and compare our analytic narratives. Studying a well-established
methodology led to the creation of a new approach, a methodology that was responsive to this particular study, its participants, and its goals.

The concept of responsive, evolving methodologies is a cornerstone of many
qualitative traditions; it is not yet widely accepted by funding agencies nor many
university researchers who have become skilled at writing grants. As the educational research culture broadens, those of us in the university community may be
able to draw on the traditions of action research and teacher research which make
such evolving methodologies both necessary and respected.

A constructivist stance would suggest that researchers, whether university-based or school-based, learn to research by doing. University-based researchers usually begin with studying research, then doing it; school-based researchers tend to begin by doing, studying as they go. By recording, discussing, and reflecting on research processes, teacher researchers can claim an intellectual tradition that values the adaptation as well as the creation of methods. While this constructivist stance may be counter to the research model currently expected of university researchers and by funding agencies, it might generate a wave of methodological creativity that benefits researchers in other fields as well. Indeed, such flexibility and invention are fundamental to some qualitative traditions. According to LeCompte and Preissle (1993), "sources and types of data are limited only by the creativity and energy of the researcher. . . . Data, then, are any kind of information which researchers can identify and accumulate to facilitate answers to their queries" (pp. 158–159).

Writing Communities

School and university writing communities have, for the most part, remained separate. At the risk of overgeneralizing, most school-based researchers do not read *Reading Research Quarterly*, and most university-based researchers do not read *Teacher Research*. Researchers in both communities write for specific audiences and purposes. But too often, rather than trying to understand each other, we talk past each other, and even belittle the writing of other discourse traditions. A thorough theoretical foundation and review of related literature is mandated in one tradition, while editors and readers expect classroom vignettes, personal feelings, and interpretation in another.

Betty has had the opportunity to participate in studies with a variety of co-researchers. She has learned that others' written versions of the classroom do not always look like her version. What to her was a dynamic home-school journal dialogue to be pondered and celebrated was, to an outsider, a task to be completed and counted. Their reports differed in language, labels, and interpretation of the lived experience. Sometimes she did not recognize her own classroom or agree with analyses. Other times, however, she and outside researchers have discovered similar or complementary findings, but have written about them in different ways, for different audiences. The latter situation broadens our understanding and connects different discourse traditions.

The point we think is critical here is that there is no single way to write about what we learn. One school district's research team generated a list of potential audiences, what content or evidence might be most convincing to each, and what products they might create from their data (Kings Bridge Road Research Team 1995). They identified twelve different audiences (e.g., students, board members, state department personnel) and developed different products for each. For example, they determined that their central office administrators wanted to know levels (including hours) of teacher involvement related to student learning (number of books read, pieces written, projects completed) and the dollars the local university was investing in the project. They wrote a one-page executive summary that included this information, made available full annual reports, and made a presentation with a policy brief handout.

The SRC funding agency OERI had a progressive process for writing. Researchers indicated what kind of written product was most logical for that project: Researchers could produce a research report (required) plus a policy brief, instructional resource, or concept paper based on intended audience and use. We encourage other funding agencies to ask the researchers what forms of reporting would be most useful to them and their constituencies and to avoid asking for reports that cannot be used for other purposes.

Potential Engagements

Many members of the educational community are deeply involved in theory *and* research *and* practice, all committed to helping learners (teachers and students) reach their full potential as human beings. If we are willing to destruct the dichotomies, without destroying individual traditions, we might begin to learn from each other, especially in the critical arena of classroom research.

For example, university researchers studying in K–12 classrooms are increasingly grappling with many of the complexities that have characterized school-based research. Research is not as concisely and neatly defined as it once was; old formulas do not fit new questions. Since the formulas never did fit action research, teacher researchers may provide helpful models. One response to the growing teacher researcher movement has been for university researchers to say, "Good for you. Now let me show you how to do research." No doubt we would learn more if we said, instead, "Good for us. Teach me how you study the complex realities of classroom life." In turn, teacher researchers have the opportunity to seek out and adapt the accumulated experience of university researchers.

Collaboration offers one of the most promising possibilities. While genuine collaboration takes time—the development of trust, shared leadership, and the negotiation of difficult issues (Allen, Buchanan, Edelsky, and Norton 1993)—it can be a structure that facilitates both divergent and convergent decision making. In our six-year collaboration, we have tried to establish an open dialogue about our roles, especially as they impact writing. By many trials and more than one error, with our colleague Barbara we have identified processes that facilitated collaboration. These processes deal with the issues this chapter raises about time, methodology, and written discourse.

We created *research time* with a variety of structures, including a paid substitute for weekly during-school data analysis sessions, weekly or biweekly work sessions at good restaurants, and week-long writing sessions at inspiring settings (see the research process appendix in Shockley et al. 1995 for details). As discussed earlier, we try to create *responsive methodologies* specific to our questions and contexts.

We entered into frequent *role discussions* concerning writing, including each writer's time, interest, strengths, weaknesses, and professional goals. We have found invaluable *interpretive dialogue*, carefully recorded analytic conversations about data that serve as oral drafts. We enjoy and study *writing models*, novel research as well as well-researched novels, and try to honor our individual voices ei-ther by identifying section authors or by writing in the lead author's voice. Lead au-thorship is based on a balance between idea generation, time spent in data collection and analysis, and actual writing. And perhaps most important, we have nurtured our *friendship* as well as our inquiry.

The SRC experience helped extend our discussions to include the dreaded "they"—as in "they won't let us" or "they said we have to." "They" turned out to be real people, not engraved policy. Anne Sweet, the NRRC project officer from OERI, was an invaluable colleague. She was supportive of teacher research, helped us modify forms (e.g., quarterly reports) to accommodate naturalistic in-quiry, invited teacher researchers to present with her, and flew Betty to Washington to set the performance indicators for the next round of research center proposals. Similarly, the Spencer Foundation has people directing the teacher research grants who are most helpful to teachers from the application process through implemen-tation, including Becky Barr and Marty Rutherford, a respected teacher researcher herself.

Almost every profession is changing rapidly, and "even those who continue to wear the same professional label survive only because they have altered what they do" (Bateson 1989, 7). Researchers exploring, and many embracing, qualitative methods are one example; the steady pilgrimage out of labs and into classrooms is another. But these "alterations" may only make off-the-rack, ready-to-wear research practices a bit more stylish. If we are really looking for the timeless, long-lasting fit of classic design, we need to tailor our research to the individual. And we need to do it, if together, at least in dialogue.

Potential Directions: A Personal Note

Where are we moving now? After nearly a decade of collaborative action research and membership on teacher research teams both large and small, where do we see ourselves heading, individually and together? A thoughtful reviewer of the initial draft of the book is responsible for this concluding section. S/he wrote,

> I'd like to see Betty and JoBeth take the same risk so many of the authors in this book do—turning a critical lens on themselves, to figure out how this amazing research ven-ture has challenged and changed their own lives as teacher researchers. . . . Challenge us to do what you've done—to take on the hard work of true collaboration between universities, government funding agencies, and public schools.

Betty is in a new and challenging research position; she is a full-time third grade teacher conducting dissertation research in her classroom. Further compli-cating the situation is the fact that she has requested JoBeth as her major professor. With JoBeth in this position, the power relationship that they had eliminated be-tween university and teacher researcher is reinstated for a time. Both have con-cerns that this process may interfere with their friendship and collaboration, but Betty insisted that she be able to continue learning from a respected mentor.

When Betty completes her Ph.D., she faces a difficult decision. Will she continue her work as a classroom teacher or as a university professor? Having spent three years at the university directing the SRC, and then returning to the classroom, she knows well how quickly one can lose touch with the realities of classroom life. She worries that moving to a university setting will mean a loss of credibility with other teacher researchers; on the other hand, the restraints of teaching limit her ability to reach other teachers and schools who request her support as researchers. Recently a parent confessed to Betty, "I would like for my child to be in your room next year, but I need to know if you will be out of the classroom as much as you were this year." Flexible time for working with teacher researchers, presenting at conferences, reflecting, reading, and writing are appealing; school structures disregard the importance of these vital professional elements.

Betty is interested in studying with other teachers the potential of research for their profession. She feels strongly that teachers should have opportunities to contribute to the educational discourse in ways that are thoughtful and rigorous and can affect policy. It will be a challenge to decide how best to continue this work.

JoBeth is ready to move beyond the divisive dichotomies that have both moved the field of literacy education and threatened to impede it. Just as both qualitative and quantitative research are important ways of knowing, and phonics is an important part of every effective whole language classroom, so too are different kinds of classroom studies valuable. She is more interested in instances where schools and universities are working well together, learning from each other, discovering both new insights about how children read and write and new ways of studying literacy development. Such collaboratives exist in many places, and their members are often publishing the results of their inquiries; a noteworthy recent example is *The Book Club Connection: Literacy Learning and Classroom Talk* (McMahon and Raphael 1997).

Second, JoBeth doesn't want to study teacher research, or teacher researchers; she wants to study children *with* teachers. During the four years she, Betty, and colleague Jim Baumann were studying the SRC (see, for example, Allen, Shockley, and Baumann 1995), JoBeth was often troubled. For one thing, this study took her out of the elementary classroom; for another, she often found herself writing the uncomfortable "they" in referring to teachers. She wants to write "we," referring to a research team. Others, mostly university researchers, have made valuable contributions to our understanding of the evolution and enactments of teacher research; these are important contributions, but not where her heart is.

Third, JoBeth would like to learn more about how to involve students and parents as collaborators. She is part of a new study with a fifth-grade teacher and two support teachers, all investigating ways of teaching students who are reading and writing significantly below grade level. They are committed to involving parents and other family members, as well as the students themselves. They will spend the year figuring out ways to do so effectively, ways based on the principles in *Engaging Children* and *Engaging Families*.

Finally, JoBeth struggles with being a teacher researcher herself. Should she join colleagues she admires who have "traded places," like University of Georgia reading professors Jim Baumann (1997), who taught second grade for a year, and Sally (Hudson-Ross and McWhorter 1995), who returned to the high school English classroom for a year? She hoped to team teach in the fifth-grade study mentioned above, but the teachers said that would not be "real," and that if the study is to be useful to teachers, it has to be conducted under the conditions of schooling. Should she study her own teaching? She tried. She kept forgetting to write in her journal. The data sit in an unexamined pile. Her research interest is not in teacher education, or even in her own teaching, but in how children who struggle in school become readers and writers.

We have fascinating and complex challenges as we evolve individually and as collaborators. We will try to take the advice of our wise colleagues. We'll also try not to take ourselves too seriously. The final chapter in this book should help.

Chapter 8—The Play

The final chapter of *Engaging Teachers* deals with many of the same issues we've addressed in this chapter, but in a fresh genre. Ann Keffer chronicles through dramatic interpretation how this new marriage of schools, university, and funding agents felt to a first-time teacher researcher.

We have some advice on how to "read" this chapter—don't just read it. Get together with others in your institution or research group, or better yet gather colleagues from across groups. Act it out. Discuss it. Revise it to fit your own experiences. Then revise it again, writing the research world the way you want to make it. Write your voices as you want the educational world to hear them from your position in public schools, universities, or funding agencies. Each of us has not only the power but the responsibility to change unproductive roles. If we dialogue, in person and through texts, with each other and with students and families, we can create a radical new script.

References

Allen, J., J. Buchanan, C. Edelsky, and G. Norton. 1992. "Teachers as 'They' at NRC: The Ethics of Collaborative and Non-collaborative Classroom Research." In *Literacy Research, Theory, and Practice: Views from Many Perspectives*, ed. C. Kinzer and D. Leu, 357-365. Chicago: National Reading Conference.

Allen, J., B. Michalove, and B. Shockley. 1993. *Engaging Children: Community and Chaos in the Lives of Young Literacy Learners*. Portsmouth, NH: Heinemann.

Allen, J. and B. Shockley. 1996. "Composing a Research Dialogue: University and School Research Communities Encountering a Cultural Shift. *Reading Research Quarterly* 31(2): 220–228.

Allen, J., B. Shockley, and J. Baumann. 1995. "Gathering 'Round the Kitchen Table: Teacher Inquiry in the NRRC School Research Consortium." *The Reading Teacher* 48(6): 526–529.

Bateson, M. C. 1989. *Composing a Life*. New York: Penguin.

Baumann, J. and G. Ivey. 1997. "Delicate Balances: Striving for Curricular and Instructional Equilibrium in a Second-grade, Literature/Strategy-based Classroom." *Reading Research Quarterly* 32(3): 244–275.

Cochran-Smith, M. and S.L. Lytle, eds. 1993. *Inside/Outside: Teacher Research and Knowledge*. New York: Teachers College Press.

Comer, J. 1988. *Maggie's American Dream: The Life and Times of a Black Family*. New York: New American Library.

Hubbard, R.S. and B.M. Power. 1993. *The Art of Classroom Inquiry: A Handbook for Teacher-researchers.* Portsmouth, NH: Heinemann.

Hudson-Ross, S. and P. McWhorter. 1995. "Going Back/Looking In: A Teacher Educator and a High School Teacher Beginning Teaching Together." *English Journal* 84(2): 46–54.

Kings Bridge Road Research Team. 1995. *Exploring Blue Highways: Literacy Reform, Change, and the Creation of Learning Communities.* New York: Teachers College Press.

LeCompte, M. and J. Preissle. 1993. *Ethnography and Qualitative Design in Educational Research.* San Diego: Academic Press.

McMahon, S. and T. Raphael. 1997. *The Book Club Connection: Literacy Learning and Classroom Talk.* New York: Teachers College Press.

Paley, V. 1990. *The Boy Who Would Be a Helicopter.* Cambridge, MA: Harvard University Press.

Shockley, B., B. Michalove, and J. Allen. 1995. *Engaging Families: Connecting Home and School Literacy Communities.* Portsmouth, NH: Heinemann.

EIGHT

Teacher Research: It's a Jungle Out There[1]

Ann Keffer

Comer Elementary School

ll summer, at the back of my mind, taking its pinch of joy out of everything I did, was the knowledge that I'd promised to have something written to take to our research group's meeting on July 31. We had to have a rough draft ready to submit to NRRC by the end of August or we wouldn't get paid.

How much did getting paid matter? To be honest, without the monetary incentive, particularly without the knowledge that four other people might not be paid if I didn't do my share, I might decide that my summer was too precious to muck up with pressure to write. I came close to deciding exactly that every time I powered up the computer, only to stare at the blank screen.

I wanted to spend my summer guiltlessly sleeping late every day, watching talk shows, and reading novels. I had managed to read some good ones, and also happened onto some interesting non-fiction: *An Anthropologist on Mars*, by Oliver Sacks; *Parting the Curtains*, by Dannye Powell; *Shadows of Forgotten Ancestors*, by Carl Sagan and Ann Druyan; and *Through a Window*, by Jane Goodall.

It was while reading the last that an analogy tripped, chortling, into my mind. Suppose, I thought, Jane Goodall had been able to persuade her chimps to keep diaries that detailed the day-to-day operation of their communities. Suppose she could get them to make little changes in this and that chimpanzee practice and record the changes and their results in the diaries. Then suppose she could talk them (or bribe them) into examining those diaries, looking for significant themes across, say, a year's worth of entries. What if she could get them to analyze those themes and write up their analyses in a format similar to that used by Jane and her fellow anthropologists?

What fun I could have developing this analogy! Its tone would certainly deviate from that expected in educational research journals, but was it reasonable to expect a chimpanzee to understand the finer points of scholarly writing?

---

1. Reprinted by permission from *Teacher Research*, Spring 1996.

There! You see? I can't resist the impulse. The following is a series of imagined conversations from which readers may draw their own parallels to teacher research.

Scene One: One side of a telephone conversation in which Ms. Goodall explains to Louis Leakey that her chimps are undertaking their own research.

"No, Doc, I'm *not* kidding. It was a bit of a lark, my asking them. No one could have been more surprised than I when they gave me that chimpanzee stare and asked if there was anything special I wanted to know about, and if I'd be supplying the materials. . . .

"No, I want them to have the freedom to focus on whatever is important to them, don't you see? I would think their very choice of topics would be revealing, wouldn't you? . . .

"Well, I went ahead and gave them pencils and paper out of my own stock, but they're going to need more, and other things too, I should think. For that matter, it would be only right to increase their ration of bananas. . . .

"No, Dr. Leakey, they're chimpanzees; I can't guarantee anything. Their priorities aren't exactly the same as ours. They've got their hands pretty full being chimps. I've seen some preliminary writings though, and they're not bad. . . .

"How should I know if scientific journals will accept their papers when I don't know half the time if they'll accept mine? . . .

"I'm sorry. I know grants don't grow on trees, and you're only trying to help. But wouldn't you think the world of ethology would welcome the chance to glimpse chimpanzee behavior from the chimp's own point of view? . . .

"Of course there are standards to maintain. I'll do my best to convey that to the chimps, but standards or no, don't you think they might have something to tell us about the world of chimpanzees? After all, who could speak with more authority on the subject? What if they do have their own way of expressing themselves? Isn't that, in itself, of interest too?"

Scene Two: A conversation in which Ms. Goodall speaks with a representative of a grant-bestowing organization.

Rep: I'm sorry, Ms. Goodall, but the proposal you sent us needs a lot of work to meet our standards.

JG: Do you realize that the grant proposal you have in your hand was conceived and written by chimpanzees?

Rep: Nevertheless. . . .

JG: I can't ask them to rewrite the proposal. It was difficult enough to begin with. You ask for these renewal applications at the worst possible times. Do you have any idea what is going on in chimpanzee communities at this time of year? Well, let me tell you, grant renewal applications are the last things on their minds. I suppose I'll just have to do it myself. Who knows if what I write will bear any relationship to what my chimps actually intend to do.

Rep: You realize the deadline is the day after tomorrow.

JG: You'll have a revision in your hands by then if it kills me, I promise.

Scene Three: A conversation between Ms. Goodall and the editor of a scientific journal.

Ed: I agree the piece is remarkable. I'm just not sure it's what our readership expects to find between our covers. They're used to a certain standard of objectivity, a certain theoretical groundedness that I'm not sure this piece lives up to.

JG: Do you realize that the manuscript you're talking about was written by chimpanzees?

Ed: Well, the very fact that they write at all is, of course, remarkable. I couldn't be more impressed. Frankly, this piece has been out to a lot of reviewers, and they are divided neatly down the middle in their response to it. Half of them praise its freshness, its honesty, its timeliness, and its clear, readable style. The other half find it wholly unsuitable for a scientific journal. I don't see how I can justify publishing it as a research article. Perhaps we could frame it more as a chimpanzee perspective piece.

JG: Publish it as a weather report for all I care, as long as you publish it.

Scene Four: A further conversation between Ms. Goodall and the representative of the grant-bestowing agency.

Rep: Ms. Goodall, I've just read your article. As a matter of fact, everyone here has read it. They all send their congratulations!

JG: My article? I don't have a recent article.

Rep: Of course you do! The one you got the chimpanzees to write.

JG: Oh, the chimpanzees' article.

Rep: Well, yes, I suppose so. Anyway, congratulations! And, by the way, Ms. Goodall, we've decided to renew your grant.

JG: Oh, thank goodness, the chimps were about to run out of pencils. Did you include bananas for them? They put a lot of time into that article, you know.

Scene Five: A conversation between Ms. Goodall and a fellow scientist, whom we will call Prof, who has read her chimpanzees' published piece.

Prof: Don't you think they're a little light on citations? Surely there is more in print concerning chimpanzee behavior than is represented in their bibliography.

JG: Maybe so, Prof, maybe so. What you have to understand is that in order to search the literature they have to leave their natural habitat, abandon their communities for days at a time, travel long distances, and master unfamiliar technologies. They take their community responsibilities very seriously. They experience guilt when they are absent from the community and someone else has to take over their role.

Prof: Well, I say if they're going to do research they should do it properly or not at all.

JG: I'll tell them you said so.

Prof: Another thing. Why on earth did they spend so much time discussing brachiation? We have all the data we could possibly want on brachiation.

JG: Well, perhaps they thought we'd like to know what *they* think about it. We've never really heard it described from their point of view before.

Prof: And the way they went on and on about food sources. There are so many more important subjects they could discuss.

JG: I guess food sources are pretty important to *them*, don't you?

Prof: Who cares what's important to them? They're our journals. We're the ones that read them. We're the ones whose livelihoods depend on publishing in them.

JG: A few of my chimps read every issue. Maybe more will, once their own work is published in them. Besides, isn't one of our main purposes to improve the lot of the animals we study? For that reason, shouldn't we care what's important to them? Maybe they'll find a way to improve their own lot. After all, by teaching them to do research, we've taught them to pay attention to what's happening every moment right in their own communities, to stop doing what doesn't further their aims, and to do more of what does. They're becoming more experimental right before my eyes. I don't mean to be immodest, but sometimes I think I may even be stimulating chimpanzee evolution.

Scene Six: A conversation between Ms. Goodall and one of the chimpanzee researchers, Gigi.

Jane: I wish the others could have come today. It's an important meeting.

Gigi: I know. They all wanted to be here, but the demands of being a full-time chimpanzee just wouldn't allow it. The community can't function right now with all of us absent at the same time.

Jane: I have news. Our grant has been renewed. We've set aside a certain amount to fund your projects. You can draw on that for supplies immediately, but I'll have to have a rough draft of another article in hand by March 1 before I can release any bananas to you.

Gigi: Frankly, Jane, I can't promise right now that our group will continue for another year. Being a chimpanzee is a high-stress occupation, you know, and we can hardly stand the thought of another year of research and writing cutting into what little leisure time we have.

Jane: I know exactly how you feel.

Gigi: Do you? Sure, you come out in the forest and pretend to be a chimp a couple times a week, but your main job is research. You expect us to do the research on top of being full-time chimpanzees.

Jane: Touché. But, Gigi, what you're doing is so important!

Gigi: You mean the research or being a chimp?

Jane: Both, of course, but specifically the research.

Gigi: You know, Fifi and I were talking, and we came up with some things chimps could try doing to discourage poaching. If we can talk the whole community into trying these new behaviors, we could compare the losses this year with those from last year and see if there's a difference. We could keep anecdotal records of what we do, how it affects our day-to-day existence, and what happens if and when we encounter any poachers. The resulting article itself might help to discourage poachers. What do you think?

Jane: I think it's a wonderful plan. You could actually affect the future of chimpanzee society.

Gigi: And that's the reason we'll continue—the chance that we might be heard, that we might make a difference. Don't get me wrong; we like getting a few extra bananas. If it were just a matter of bananas, though, you'd need a lot more than you have to get us to carry out these projects and write these articles. We'd much rather just groom each other and relax in the sun.

References

Goodall, J. 1990. *Through a Window: My Thirty Years with the Chimpanzees of Gombe.* Boston: Houghton Mifflin.

Keffer, A. (1996). Teacher research: It's a Jungle Out There. *Teacher Research: The Journal of Classroom Inquiry*, 3(2), p. 5–11.

Powell, D. 1995. *Parting the Curtains.* New York: Anchor Books.

Sacks, O. 1995. *An Anthropologist on Mars: Seven Paradoxical Tales.* New York: Knopf.

Sagan, C. and A. Druyan. 1992. *Shadows of Forgotten Ancestors: A Search for Who We Are.* New York: Random House.

APPENDIX A

Preliminary Research Questions of the School Research Consortium

SRC Studies and Research Questions, Year One

1. "What is the role of discussion in middle school readers' development of strategies for aesthetic reading?"—Dera Weaver.
2. "How will students who are given an opportunity to participate in generating their own curriculum respond? How will involvement in this activity affect their motivation to learn?"—Patti McWhorter, Barbara Jarrard, Sue Lee, Mindi Rhoades, and Buddy Wiltcher, Cedar Shoals High.
3. "How does researching, writing, and artistically designing a personal history book affect the self-esteem, developmental writing achievement, expressive skills, motivation for learning, and sense of cultural pride of fourth- and fifth-grade African-American students?"—Maxine Easom, David Harvell, and Gordon Eisenman, Fourth Street Elementary.
4. "What effects will corresponding with a pen pal about literature representing various cultures have upon students' racial attitudes, cultural awareness, and ethnic identity?"—Valerie L. Garfield, Chattahoochee Elementary; Susan Hollingsworth, Fourth Street Elementary.
5. "How does analyzing transcripts of video-taped story discussions result in informed reflection on second-grade students' thinking, listening, and reading, and on eighth-grade students' metacognitive thinking?"—Georgiana Sumner, Alps Road Elementary; Johni Mathis, Burney-Harris-Lyons Middle; Michelle Commeyras, UGA.
6. "Does developing confidence as a writer encourage confidence as a teacher of writing, and how does being an active writer affect us as readers? Will becoming part of an adult community of writers enable us to help children when they encounter problems with their writing?"—Debby Wood, Leah Mattison, Shelley Carr, and Ann Keffer, Comer Elementary; Randi Stanulis, UGA.
7. "When elementary and high school students write (pen pal letters) and speak or read aloud (pen pal videos) to one another, how does the quality of their written and oral language change over time, and what are the implications for early parental training?"—Emily Carr, Fourth Street Elementary; Sally Hudson-Ross, Cedar Shoals High.

8. "What can I do to prompt genuine conversation about literature, and does that conversation change if the partner is a peer rather than an adult?"—Beth Tatum, Cedar Shoals High.

9. "How will in-class discussions and activities designed to focus on key thinking skills influence aptitude scores, learning attitudes, and the ability to engage in general academic tasks demonstrating problem solving skills and strategies?"—Vicki K. Krugman, Fourth Street Elementary.

10. "How does an intensive concentration of poetry in a third-grade whole language classroom affect the reading abilities and engagement of African-American students working cooperatively in small groups?"—Carrie Gantt and Linda Smith, Fourth Street Elementary.

11. "Will at-risk ninth graders read more and improve their attitudes toward fiction and biographies when provided titles that interest them?"—Shu-Hsien Chen, UGA; Dana MacDougald, Cedar Shoals High; Melvin Bowie, UGA.

12. "Will practice writing, solving, and sharing student-made word problems help relieve student anxiety about solving word problems in testing environments, and increase their understanding of mathematical concepts?"—Sharon L. MacDonald, Comer Elementary.

13. "Can students learn to recognize and incorporate elements of a story into their own writing and retellings after hearing and viewing several versions of a fairy tale, and will students demonstrate increased self-esteem and motivation for learning and enhanced social skills through participation in this multi-age project?"—Jane Holman, Christine Fuentes, and Nancy Baumann, Barnett Shoals Elementary.

14. "What impact will inclusion of multiethnic literature have on students' self concept, academic performance in English, attitude toward reading, attitude toward Cedar Shoals (sense of belonging), and understanding and acceptance of others' cultures?"—Louise Neal, Cedar Shoals High.

15. "Will reading-writing journals serve to bridge home and school in a tangible way for children from drug-abusive backgrounds?"—Karen Hankins, Whit Davis Elementary.

16. "By team teaching science in a fourth-grade classroom, using the inclusion model for meeting the needs of the Special Education students, we wonder how writing in science journals and involving students in discussions during science circle will impact their test scores in the area of science."—Jodi P. Weber and Christine McKinney, Fourth Street Elementary.

17. "What are the benefits of a writing partnership on second- and fifth-grade students' attitudes toward and participation in the writing process?"—Wanda Wright, Jewel Moore, Pat White, and Helene Hooten, Gaines Elementary.